CLASSIC
STEAM
TRAINS

NORTH AMERICAN & INTERNATIONAL ENGINES

© 2007 by The Foundry Creative Media Company Ltd

This 2007 edition published by Barnes & Noble, Inc.,
by arrangement with The Foundry Creative Media Company Limited.

Publisher and Creative Director: Nick Wells
Art Director: Mike Spender
Layout Design: Vanessa Green
Production: Chris Herbert
Thanks to: Colin Nash, Erica Heisman, Toria Lyle, Chris Herbert, Lucy Robins (original layout)

With special thanks to Brian Solomon for his invaluable contribution to the text and use of pictures from the Brian Solomon collection.

Colin Garratt (author) Almost 40 years ago, Colin abandoned a promising commercial career to document, on color film,
the 'Last Steam Locomotives of the World'. This unique odyssey – which continues apace – has taken him to more than 50 countries
and some of the remotest places on earth. Colin has written and illustrated some 60 books on railroads, travel and photography,
including his autobiography. He is the Director of Milepost 92½, picture library and photographers to the railroad industry.
Milepost 92½ also conserves and markets Colin's collection as well as the collections of other outstanding railroad photographers.

Milepost 92½, Newton Harcourt, Leicestershire, LE8 9FH, United Kingdom
studio@railphotolibrary.com / www.railphotolibrary.com

All pictures courtesy of the **Milepost 92$^1/_2$ Collection** (see above) with the exception of the following:
Arthur Huneke: 7 (t), 12–13, 15–16, 18–19, 21–22, 35, 39, 40–41, 43, 46, 50–59, 64–66, 73–75, 82–83, 132–33, 138, 184–85, 188
The Brian Solomon Collection: 6, 7 (b), 17, 29, 60, 67–68, 77, 84–91, 94, 101–02, 106, 120, 123–24, 140–41
The Ron Ziel Collection: 34, 36–38

ISBN-13: 978-0-7607-8898-1
ISBN-10: 0-7607-8898-7

Printed and bound in China

1 3 5 7 9 10 8 6 4 2

CLASSIC
STEAM
TRAINS

NORTH AMERICAN & INTERNATIONAL ENGINES

COLIN GARRATT

BARNES & NOBLE

NEW YORK

$\mathcal{C}$ONTENTS

INTRODUCTION

In North America, the steam era was a colorful and varied time for railroad history. The railroad network consisted of dozens of overlapping regional systems, which competed fiercely with one another for freight and passenger traffic. Every railroad had its individual philosophy for motive power, and each worked with locomotive manufacturers in the design and construction of specialized machines. As a result, there was a tremendous variety of locomotive styles and types. No two railroads' locomotives looked or performed precisely the same.

In the nineteenth century, dozens of small manufacturers had thrived, with the giant of locomotive manufacturing, Baldwin Locomotive Works, constructing more than 18,000 locomotives prior to 1900. In the twentieth century, most production was the result of three large commercial builders, with Philadelphia-based Baldwin remaining the dominant and largest producer. After 1900, the American Locomotive Company (Alco) was formed by the consolidation of a variety of smaller manufacturers, among them New York State-based Schenectady Locomotive Works, and Brooks Locomotive Works. From about 1915, the Lima Locomotive Works of Lima, Ohio, emerged as a serious competitor to Baldwin and Alco in the manufacture of road locomotives. To gain a competitive edge, it pushed important innovation in American locomotive design, most significantly introducing the concept of "Superpower" with the 2-8-4 Berkshire type in the mid-1920s. Although not new to locomotive building, since 1885 Lima had primarily focused on the construction of small industrial locomotives such as the geared Shay type. Other companies, such as H.K. Porter, had exclusively built small switchers and industrial types.

In addition to the commercial builders, a few railroads in the twentieth century designed, refined, and manufactured their own steam power, notably the Pennsylvania Railroad (P.R.R.) at its Juniata Shops in Altoona, Pennsylvania; and Norfolk & Western at its Roanoke, Virginia, shops. P.R.R. was the first to adopt a scientific approach in locomotive design, using its Altoona test plant to measure and maximize locomotive output and employ calculated innovation and refinement. It was also the first to adopt standardized types with interchangeable parts,

rather than use a small order of custom-built machines. When P.R.R. settled on a standard type, it tended to order nearly identical locomotives by the hundreds.

Steam locomotive development in America resulted in a constant but gradual enlargement of the conventional reciprocating locomotive. From the formative period in the 1830s and 1840s, to the end of steam, the trend was toward ever larger, heavier, and more powerful locomotives. For much of the nineteenth century, the 4-4-0 was the dominant type, yet later versions were as much as three times heavier than the earliest. By the late-nineteenth century, 2-6-0 Moguls, 4-6-0 Ten Wheelers, and 2-8-0 Consolidations had joined the ranks of the 4-4-0 American. In the 1880s and 1890s, widespread application of several key innovations resulted in a demand for significantly more powerful locomotives, which produced a host of new types. The automatic air brake and automatic block signaling permitted the safe operation of much longer, heavier, and faster trains, while the development of steel-framed, and later steel-bodied, railroad cars substantially increased the weight of trains.

In addition to greater power, greater efficiency was sought. From the late 1880s to around the First World War, many lines bought compound locomotives. These used various configurations of high- and low-pressure cylinders to reuse exhausted steam and maximize its use to improve thermal efficiency. The most notable and most common type of compound was the articulated Mallet, which had originated in continental Europe for narrow-gauge use. It was adapted after 1904 for heavy American service. The advent of superheating was more significant and nearly universal in application – from about 1910 onward, most new locomotives were fitted with superheaters that recirculated steam through the fire tubes, which supercharged it, greatly improving the engine's efficiency.

In the 1920s, the insatiable need for greater power resulted in a new generation of even mightier machines. Alco developed three-cylinder simple types—the largest were 4-12-2s for Union Pacific—while Lima introduced its aforementioned Superpower concept, which embraced a large enough firebox and boiler to supply sufficient steam to maintain high output at

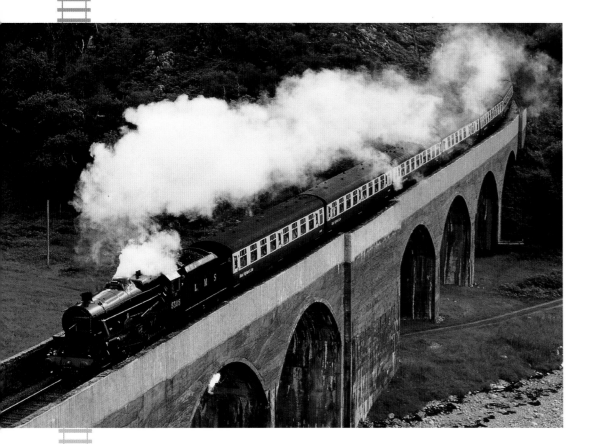

and various P.R.R. designs styled by Raymond Loewy. Of greater technological significance were refinements such as roller bearings, reciprocating parts manufactured from new lightweight steel alloys, welded boiler construction, and precision counterbalancing. A few railroads experimented with innovations such as watertube boilers and engines with extremely high boiler pressure. Pennsylvania Railroad developed several enormously fast and powerful split drive "Duplex" types. And there was nominal interest in development of steam turbine types. During this period, the steam locomotive achieved its most impressive characteristics. Some of the fastest, the most powerful, and by far the largest locomotives were built.

In common with America, the development of British steam locomotives was both innovative and dramatic. Throughout the nineteenth century and the first quarter of the twentieth, Britain's railroads were comprised of numerous private companies. Again, in common with America, a huge variety of private builders came into existence to produce locomotives for the mainline companies, industry, and an ever developing overseas trade, as Britain exported its Industrial Revolution across the world. The first steam locomotives in America were British-built.

higher speeds. During this time, the simple articulated type was refined; this resembled the Mallet with two sets of cylinders and running gear below a common boiler, but did not use the compound arrangement, and all cylinders operated at high pressure. Improvements to articulated design not only permitted vastly more powerful locomotives, but also allowed them to operate at higher sustained speeds than the early Mallets.

The final phase of development was in reaction to the advent of the diesel-electric. A number of railroads introduced streamlined steam locomotives. Some used shrouds designed in wind tunnels to reduce air drag, but most simply embodied a modern aesthetic intended to impress the public. The best known of the streamliners were New York Central's Dreyfus-designed J-3a Hudsons, Milwaukee Road's A1 Atlantics and F7 Hudsons styled by Otto Kuhler for service on the Hiawatha,

However, in Britain all of the large mainline companies designed and built their own locomotives in their own works, giving rise to famous railroad towns such as Crewe, Derby, Doncaster, and Swindon. But the biggest difference between American and British locomotive practice was one which persisted throughout the steam age, and that was the size and power of the locomotives at any given period; British locomotives, by comparison with America's, were diminutive. Freight trains in Britain, up to the beginning of the twentieth century, were largely in the hands of inside-cylinder 0-6-0s, a

CLASSIC
STEAM
TRAINS

NORTH AMERICAN & INTERNATIONAL ENGINES

COLIN GARRATT

BARNES & NOBLE

NEW YORK

CONTENTS

form of engine introduced in the 1830s; the 0-8-0 was a logical development, but it flowered on relatively few railroads. The 2-8-0 appeared in 1903, and this form of locomotive was to remain the prevalent freight hauler until the end of steam. For passenger trains, Singles or 2-4-0s held sway until the last quarter of the nineteenth century, when the inside-cylinder 4-4-0 assumed prevalence. The first years of the twentieth century became known as the Atlantic Era, with 4-6-0s emerging simultaneously, and these, by the 1920s, had evolved into the Pacific. Apart from the comparative sizes of similar types, British evolution terminated with the Pacific. America graduated to Hudson 4-6-4s and 4-8-4 Northerns, while British trusty 2-8-0s saw their American equivalents gravitating to Mikado 2-8-2s, Berkshire 2-8-4s, Santa Fe 2-10-2s, and Texas 2-10-4s, in addition to big semi-articulated Mallets which culminated in the 520-ton Union Pacific 2-8-8-4 Big Boys.

While American railroad companies remained in private hands, the grouping of Britain's railroads in 1923 combined 120 separate organizations into just four: the L.M.S., L.N.E.R., Great Western, and the Southern. Known as the "Big Four", these companies existed for exactly 25 years before the railroads were nationalized into British Railways. Under the big four, the steam locomotive reached its zenith; this period coincided with the streamlined era, and the flamboyance of the L.M.S. Coronations and L.N.E.R. A4s has never been bettered. Nationalization found the railroad with literally hundreds of different types, many dating back to the pre-grouping years, so a program of 12 standard steam types was drawn up, which was intended to cover the entire country. They embraced all categories of traffic from express passenger to branch and cross-country operations. All were designated as Mixed Traffic designs with the exception of the 9F Heavy Mineral 2-10-0,

although, paradoxically, these turned out to be equally at home on express passenger work with speeds of 90 mph being reported.

By the time the BR Standards were introduced, America was rapidly running down steam in favor of diesel and, by 1960, steam had been purged from all American Class 1 operations. Following suit, in 1956 the British government announced a modernization plan under which steam was to be phased out. Sadly, despite firm predictions that steam would survive until the end of the twentieth century, after a running-down period of 10 years, the last fire was dropped in August 1968, and the steam train became extinct in the land of its birth. Fortunately there were many who were not prepared to face a world without steam trains. Well over 2,000 steam locomotives have been preserved in Britain and some 1,800 in America. Many of these now operate on preserved lines and on mainline excursions.

Colin Garratt, Milepost 92½

PASSENGER LOCOMOTIVES

Through much of the nineteenth century, American operators were content to assign 4-4-0 "American" types to passenger service. However, by the latter part of the century some railroads were looking to operate significantly faster express trains, and, as trains got heavier and longer, bigger locomotives were needed. The American steam locomotive increased its weight more than tenfold and, in a mere 80 years, its power twentyfold. The 4-4-2 Atlantic was built as an express passenger engine from about 1895 to 1910. Mountainous lines adopted the 4-6-0 as a passenger hauler.

In the first decade of the twentieth century, the 4-6-2 Pacific matured as a heavy passenger locomotive. Some lines developed the 4-8-2 Mountain for passenger service, especially in graded territory. In the 1920s, the advent of Superpower produced both the 4-6-4 Hudson type and the 4-8-4 Northern. One of the last developments was Pennsylvania's class T1 4-4-4-4 Duplex type.

The final 50 years of steam development saw the greatest distinction between British and American practice. In Britain, the Pacific did not become established until the 1920s and 1930s, and even then only with two of the big four companies. Nothing bigger occurred, with the exception of a few Mikados, built by the L.N.E.R., but even this bold step was retrenched and all examples were rebuilt into Pacifics.

STRASBURG RAILROAD

4-4-0

The 4-4-0 was not only the most popular type of locomotive of the nineteenth century, but also remained a standard type into the twentieth century. Some lines such as the Pennsylvania Railroad continued to order new 4-4-0s for light passenger services well after larger, more powerful types had been developed for express passenger trains. P.R.R.'s D16b class, built between 1900 and 1908, turned out to be its most popular class of 4-4-0—ultimately P.R.R. operated 262 of them. Many D16s were later modernized with superheating equipment and continued to operate in daily service until the mid-1940s. Pennsylvania Railroad Class D16sb No. 1223 was lucky and escaped the scrapper's torch. Today, it is preserved at the Railroad Museum of Pennsylvania in Strasburg.

G.W.R. CITY

4-4-0

In Britain, in the transition from William Dean to G.J. Churchward on the G.W.R., several of the traditional Great Western double-framed 4-4-0s were rebuilt, with the American-inspired taper boiler allied to the Belgian Belpaire firebox which was to become the hallmark of Churchward's designs. Ten new express 4-4-0s of similar appearance were ordered from Swindon works in 1903 and named after cities served by the G.W.R. They quickly proved to be exceedingly fast machines and recorded many high-speed runs, but their lasting fame is down to No. 3440 *City of Truro*, which raced down Wellington bank in Somerset on May 9th, 1904 at the head of the *Ocean Mails Express* and was unofficially timed at 102.3 mph.

PENNSYLVANIA RAILROAD CLASS E2 AND D16

4-4-2 and 4-4-0

In the 1890s, the 4-4-2 Atlantic evolved from the 4-4-0 American. The addition of a radial trailing truck permitted a significantly larger boiler, making possible a much more powerful locomotive, especially at high speeds. By design, the 4-4-2 type was often built for express passenger service. As America's premier passenger carrier, the Pennsylvania Railroad owned more passenger locomotives than most smaller railroads' total locomotive fleets. Between 1899 and 1914, P.R.R. acquired nearly 600 Atlantics. The finest examples were the E6s Atlantics. This shot taken in the mid-1980s shows a former P.R.R. E2 Atlantic and a D16 American both preserved and restored for excursion services.

P.R.R. DOUBLE HEADER

4-4-2 and 4-4-0

It was a real event in the mid-1980s when this Pennsylvania Railroad E2-class Atlantic—dressed up as the famous 7002—made an appearance with P.R.R. Class D16sb No. 1233 in mainline excursion service. Although the Atlantic no longer runs, it is now proudly displayed at the Railroad Museum of Pennsylvania at Strasburg.

C.&E.I. NO. 153

4-6-0

Chicago & Eastern Illinois No. 153 is classic example of a nineteenth-century locomotive built to twentieth-century dimensions. By 1900, the size of locomotives had grown to handle significantly heavier trains, yet the technology had not evolved to make the locomotives more efficient. This heavy 4-6-0 has tall drivers, yet uses inside valve gear, D slide valves and saturated steam. Later passenger locomotives would use superheated steam (which would require cylindrical piston valves), larger pistons, and thus outside valve gear and heavier drive rods, as well as a larger boiler needing a radial trailing truck to support a much heavier firebox.

P.R.R. K4S

4-6-2

The Pennsylvania Railroad developed the K4s 4-6-2 Pacific in 1914. It blended the best characteristics of an earlier class of Pacific with its already successful E6s Atlantic to produce a more powerful and more efficient passenger locomotive. Like many P.R.R. steam locomotives, the K4s used a Belpaire firebox, a feature readily distinguished by its squared-off boxy appearance at the cab end of the boiler. Never a railroad to rush into anything too quickly, P.R.R. put the prototype K4s Pacific through extensive tests before beginning mass production in 1917. By 1924, the railroad had built 324 K4s locomotives at its Juniata Shops in Altoona, Pennsylvania. The K4s type finished out its days in New York & Long Branch suburban service in 1957.

LONG ISLAND NO. 39

4-6-0

Long Island Rail Road's G5s Ten-Wheeler was an unusually late example of the 4-6-0 wheel arrangement. In the nineteenth century, the 4-6-0 had been a popular type for heavy freight locomotives in America, and used in mountain service. By contrast, P.R.R.'s G5s was developed by the Pennsylvania Railroad in 1920 for suburban passenger service, and was among the last 4-6-0s built new. L.I.R.R.'s G5s looked very much like P.R.R. locomotives, but its boxy Belpaire firebox and keystone number plate are instant giveaways.

CANADIAN NATIONAL CLASS J-4-D

4-6-2

Some locomotive designers made every effort to produce balanced if utilitarian designs. Careful consideration was given to the shape and placement of key appliances such as steam and sand domes, feedwater heaters, and air pumps, in order to keep their machines as attractive as possible without the need for streamlined shrouding or other superfluous equipment. The Canadian National J-4-d Pacific appears to be an exception to this philosophy; its awkwardly arranged equipment leads to not just a utilitarian appearance, but also general disharmony. The class was built during the First World War, so perhaps the global tensions and feelings of chaos permeated the minds of the locomotive's designers.

P.R.R. ATLANTIC

4-4-2

The Atlantic type sat in the limelight for just a few years before it was surpassed by the Pacific as America's standard long-distance passenger locomotive. Bumped from premier assignments by the 1920s, some Atlantics were reassigned to secondary long-distance passenger trains and suburban services. As they were built for speed and were not sufficiently powerful to move the heavier trains of the post-First World War period, however, Atlantics were not well suited to freight service, branch-line work, or even work-train service.

LONG ISLAND G5 NO. 20

4-6-0

Pennsylvania Railroad's Long Island Rail Road affiliate operated an intensive suburban passenger service on its namesake. Many of its locomotives were either handed down from its parent company or specifically built for it by P.R.R.'s Juniata Shops. Pennsylvania Railroad was the nation's largest passenger carrier, and in the 1920s its K4s Pacifics and E6s Atlantic were busy handling long-distance assignments. It specially designed the G5s 4-6-0 Ten-Wheeler for suburban working and built 90 for its own services and 31 for Long Island Rail Road. L.I.R.R. No. 20 is seen here in the early 1950s. P.R.R. began electrifying L.I.R.R. with third rail in the early twentieth century. Today, Long Island Rail Road, long since separated from P.R.R., is largely electrified and the days of steam long forgotten.

G.W.R. CASTLE

4-6-0

In Britain, unlike Churchward, Charles Collett was not a groundbreaking engineer, choosing instead to build steadily on his predecessor's designs within the G.W.R. tradition. His Castle class of 1923 is a case in point, being a larger and more powerful version of Churchward's four-cylinder Star class of 1906. This was achieved by fitting a bigger boiler and cylinders to the Star chassis, producing a locomotive that was to become the G.W.R.'s principal express type for the next 35 years. One hundred and seventy-one locomotives were constructed in total, including several rebuilt from Stars, the final Castle emerging from Swindon, Wiltshire, in 1950.

FLYING SCOTSMAN
L.N.E.R. A3
4-6-2

Arguably the most famous locomotive in the world, No. 4472 *Flying Scotsman* was the first Pacific to be built by the L.N.E.R. in 1923. It hauled the 10 am service of the same name from King's Cross on its inaugural run of 392 miles to Edinburgh in 1928, the longest non-stop journey in the world. The same engine hit the headlines again in 1934 by achieving the first authenticated 100 mph by a steam locomotive. Small wonder that when it was retired in 1963, it was purchased for preservation and has since led an eventful life travelling the world.

S.R. LORD NELSON
4-6-0

A peculiarity of the Lord Nelsons lay in the setting of the crank angles by which the engine gave eight exhausts per revolution of the driving wheels instead of four, resulting in a very soft blast and even torque. They required skillful firing to give the best performance, but were enormously improved by Oliver Bulleid, who fitted the class with the Lemaitre five-jet multiple blastpipe and larger piston valves. The class worked until 1962, when happily No. 30850 *Lord Nelson* was selected for preservation in Britain's National Collection.

CANADIAN PACIFIC CLASS G-2-S

4-6-2

Canadian Pacific favored the 4-6-2 Pacific type for passenger services until it adopted the 4-6-4 Hudson in 1929. By contrast, C.P.R.'s competitor C.N.R., which had also employed large numbers of Pacifics, embraced the 4-8-4 Northern instead of the Hudson. Here, on September 16, 1945, Canadian Pacific No. 2548 Class G-2 Pacific pauses at Nesbitt, Manitoba. Ahead of the smokestack is an Elesco feedwater heater, a device introduced to supply preheated water to the boiler and thus minimize heat loss and improve engine efficiency.

S.R. SCHOOLS

4-4-0

The constricted loading gauge of Britain's Tonbridge–Hastings line had always imposed severe restrictions on locomotive design, ruling out the larger classes for which its train loadings called. Richard Maunsell's masterpiece, the Schools, or V, class 4-4-0 of 1930, was tailored to the requirements of the route. With three cylinders powering four coupled wheels, it had all the power needed within a short frame length, and its angled-in profile fitted within the width restrictions of the tunnels. In all, 40 were built and named after famous private and public schools.

N.Y.C. HUDSON NO. 324

4-6-4

In 1927, New York Central was the first to adopt the 4-6-4 type, which was named in honor of the Hudson River, that body of water whose shores Central's "Water Level Route" hugs between New York City and Albany. In 1934, New York Central made another historic first when it experimentally applied aerodynamic streamlined shrouds to an Alco-built J1-class Hudson. During the 1930s, New York Central's chief engineer Paul Kiefer worked with Alco and continued to refine the Hudson, resulting in the superb J-3a class. The last 10 of these were built in 1938 and exquisitely styled by Henry Dreyfus, bought in conjunction with Central's re-equipped lightweight Twentieth Century Limited. One of these beautiful Dreyfus Hudsons is seen here racing northward along the Hudson at Manitou, New York.

L.M.S. PRINCESS ROYAL

4-6-2

The first two "Princess Royal" Pacifics emerged from Crewe works, Cheshire, in 1933 and fulfilled their designer's expectations. No. 6201 *Princess Elizabeth* set an impressive record in 1936, hauling a seven-coach train nonstop from London to Glasgow in under six hours, an unprecedented feat. Fittingly, this locomotive has been preserved, together with the first of the production batch, No. 6203 *Princess Margaret Rose*, and both have been active on mainline excursions in recent years.

L.M.S. JUBILEE 5XP

4-6-0

The L.M.S. "Jubilee" 4-6-0s were conceived by William Stanier as a taper boiler development of the existing Patriot class, and 79 engines were ordered straight off the drawing board in 1934. Initially, poor steaming compromised their performance, however, and it took three years to find a cure. Once this was remedied, the Jubilees were transformed and performed superbly on the former Midland mainlines from London to Manchester and over the Settle and Carlisle route. In all, 191 engines were built, and it was not until 1967 that the final three were retired from the Leeds Holbeck shed.

L.M.S. PRINCESS CORONATION
4-6-2 (Streamlined)

Spurred on by the records set by the L.N.E.R.'s high-speed streamlined services, the L.M.S. responded in July 1937 by introducing the Coronation Scot service, maintaining a regular six-hour London to Glasgow schedule. Simultaneously, William Stanier produced his finest design, the Princess Coronation four-cylinder Pacifics. The first five entered service with stylish blue-and-silver streamlined casings to match the new trains, and soon showed their prodigious power and speed. On a special run from Euston, London, to Crewe, Cheshire, in 1937, No. 6220 *Coronation* set a new British speed record of 114 mph.

L.M.S. PRINCESS CORONATION
4-6-2 (Non-streamlined)

After the first 10 streamlined L.M.S. Pacifics had entered service, a further five were outshopped in non-streamlined form, revealing the handsome and powerful profile that lay beneath the casing. On a test run in February 1939, No. 6234 *Duchess of Abercorn* showed just how powerful they were. Hauling a 20-coach, 605-tonne train from Crewe to Glasgow and back, she recorded an indicated horsepower of 3,330 while climbing Beattock bank, a power output from a steam locomotive that has never been matched in Britain. All the streamliners lost their casings after the Second World War but three of these magnificent machines have been preserved.

S.P.&S. NO. 700

4-8-4

Spokane, Portland & Seattle was jointly owned by Northern Pacific and Great Northern. They built the railroad with a low grade line that provided both N.P. and G.N. better access to Portland, Oregon. S.P.&S. No. 700 was one of three modern 4-8-4s built for the railroad by Baldwin in 1938. These oiler burners were similar in design to late-era Northerns built for Northern Pacific. No. 700 worked both passenger and freight services. Following its retirement in 1956, No. 700 was placed in a public park in Portland, Oregon, along with Southern Pacific No. 4449. In 1990, S.P.&S. 700 was restored to operation and has been occasionally used for mainline passenger excursions.

SOUTHERN PACIFIC GS-4

4-8-4

Connecting San Francisco and Los Angeles were Southern Pacific's famous *Daylight* passenger trains and the exclusive overnight sleeper known as *The Lark*. When the new streamlined *Daylights* were introduced in the mid-1930s, they provided more than mere transportation; they conveyed passengers in both comfort and style. To haul its luxury streamliners, Southern Pacific ordered specially designed and exquisitely styled Lima-built 4-8-4s. The finest of these were the GS-4-class ones built in 1941. In later years, some of the streamlined 4-8-4s received a Spartan treatment; parts of the shrouding were removed, and the locomotives were painted black instead of in the trademark red, orange, and silver *Daylight* livery. One of these latter-day adorned GS-4s works on the Southern Pacific Coast line with the streamlined *Daylight*.

STREAMLINED PACIFIC

4-6-2

The first American streamlined steam locomotives used shrouding developed in wind tunnel tests to reduce air drag. Later streamlining treatments were intended purely for aesthetic value. These were styled to make the locomotives appear modern and to conceal unsightly equipment with visually appealing sheet metal. In 1940, industrial designer Otto Kuhler provided futuristic streamlining for Lehigh Valley, which dressed up some of its 4-6-2 Pacifics—built in the mid-1920s—for service on its flagship *Black Diamond*. The luxury train traversed the length of Lehigh Valley's mainline between New York City and Buffalo by way of Allentown, and Wilkes Barre, Pennsylvania.

READING 2102

4-8-4

In 1945, when most American railroads were purchasing diesels, the Reading Company made the unusual move and chose to build its own 4-8-4 Northerns. These were essentially re-manufactured locomotives built with the boilers and fireboxes from Reading's I-10sa class 2-8-0 Consolidations. Known as the T-1 class, these 4-8-4s primarily worked heavy coal trains. In the late 1950s, Reading Company finally converted to diesels, but retained five of its T-1 Class 4-8-4s for excursion work and for several years used them on its famous "Reading Rambles" around its system in eastern Pennsylvania.

NORFOLK & WESTERN
4-8-4

Best known as a heavy coal hauler, Norfolk and Western also had passenger trains which were characterized by its streamlined Powhaten Arrow, typically hauled by its magnificent J Class 4-8-4s. Here number 611 of the class is seen running in preservation at Blue Ridge, Virginia, on September 4th 1982.

SOUTHERN PACIFIC
4-8-2

Southern Pacific's suburban passenger trains working between San Francisco and San Jose were always known as Commutes, unlike suburban trains in the eastern United States that were often described as commuter trains. By the mid-1950s, Southern Pacific had dieselized the majority of its long-distance services and reassigned some of its late-era passenger locomotives to the Commutes. The 4-8-2 Mountain type was ideally suited for heavy passenger work, especially in graded territory. As Southern Pacific crossed a major mountain grade just about everywhere it went, it had a substantial fleet of 4-8-2s.

SOUTHERN PACIFIC GOLDEN STATE

4-8-4

This is one of Southern Pacific's famous GS-4 4-8-4s works trains, No. 373 in the early 1950s. Among the finest 4-8-4s were Southern Pacific's magnificent semi-streamlined Class GS-4s built by Lima in 1941. These were among the most advanced reciprocating steam locomotive designs. They featured four pairs of 80-inch driving wheels powered by 26 x 32-inch cylinders and a high-capacity boiler working at 300 psi. While styled for service on Southern Pacific's famous *Daylight* passenger trains, the GS-4s were technically dual-traffic locomotives and, in addition to occasional freight work, often hauled Southern Pacific's secondary named passenger trains.

L.M.S. REBUILT ROYAL SCOT

4-6-0

The entry into service in 1927 of the first 50 "Royal Scots" at last gave the L.M.S. a worthy express passenger locomotive. Twenty more came from Derby works in 1930. An additional locomotive was built with an experimental super-pressure boiler, but suffered a fatal tube burst while on trial. Stanier fitted its chassis with a large taper boiler with double blastpipe and smokestack to form the prototype for rebuilding the rest of the class. It was a process that took until 1955 to complete, but it transformed good engines into excellent ones. The rebuilt Scots delivered the highest power output per tonne of any British 4-6-0, outclassing even the G.W.R. Kings passenger trains.

L.I.R.R. NO. 21

4-6-0

Back in the early 1950s, few commuters appreciated the experience of traveling to work behind a Long Island Rail Road G5s 4-6-0. In those days, the passenger cars were not air-conditioned and, to keep cool in summer, the windows were left open—exposing passengers to cinders and ash. Regular steam operations ended on the Long Island Rail Road in 1955. Today, modern electrified multiple units treat L.I.R.R. passengers to air-conditioned cars and cushioned seats. But are complaints fewer and the commuters happier? By contrast, the luxury of traveling behind a G5s Ten-Wheeler operating with vintage cars would be an attraction for which thousands would gladly pay today. In May 2005, $800,000 was presented to the Railroad Museum of Long Island to restore L.I.R.R. G5s No. 39 to service. With luck, some day old 39 may run again.

LEHIGH VALLEY CAMELBACK

4-6-0

Lehigh Valley 4-6-0 Ten-Wheeler No. 801 is an interesting machine for several reasons. Not only is it a anthracite burner with the shallow, wide Wootten firebox and Camelback dual cab arrangement, but it is a classic example of a Baldwin Vauclain compound type. Using double expansion of steam with high- and low-pressure cylinders, a compound engine improves upon the thermal efficiency of the engine. Baldwin's Samuel M. Vauclain developed a four-cylinder non-articulated compound system using high- and low-pressure cylinders on both sides of the engine. Although this system improved engine efficiency, it also increased maintenance costs. When wages in America rose steeply during the First World War period, high-maintenance compounds fell out of favor. Some were rebuilt as simple engines; others were simply scrapped.

BALTIMORE & OHIO PACIFIC

4-6-2

A smartly kept Baltimore & Ohio 4-6-2 Pacific marches out of Grafton, West Virginia, in the early 1950s, with a secondary passenger train in tow—probably the nameless No. 11. Like many secondary passenger trains of the period, this one has lots of "head-end" traffic—United States Mail, express shipments, and small packages. Head-end traffic often generated more revenue than carrying passengers. By 1970, not only was the Pacific a memory, but so, too, was the head-end traffic, and all too often the scheduled passenger train. In 1971, a few remaining passenger routes were conveyed to Amtrak. The steam locomotives and passenger trains are gone, but Grafton remains a vital railroad town; the lines there now primarily serve as a conduit for heavy coal trains. The coal is used to generate commercial electricity or sold for export, while the locomotives that haul it run on diesel fuel.

CHESAPEAKE & OHIO CLASS L-1

4-6-4

After the Second World War, when most American railroads were placing large orders for new diesels, coal-hauler Chesapeake & Ohio maintained its loyalty to steam. It rebuilt five 4-6-2 Pacifics into modern 4-6-4 Hudsons in 1946 and 1947. These were equipped with modern refinements such as rotary cam poppet valves and roller bearings, and four of them were streamlined with stainless-steel shrouding. Although late in the game, these were not the last streamlined steam locomotives in America. Norfolk & Western continued to order new streamlined J-class 4-8-4s until 1950. Today, the last C.&O. Hudson can be seen as a static display in Baltimore, Maryland, at the Baltimore & Ohio Railroad Museum, while the only remaining N&W J-class, the famous 611, is displayed in Roanoke, Virginia.

FREIGHT LOCOMOTIVES

In the formative years, American freight trains were neither significantly heavier nor much faster than passenger trains; as a result, until the Civil War period, most lines were content to use the standard 4-4-0 to move both freight and passengers. After the Civil War, freight trains grew in both length and weight, and freight locomotives grew in size accordingly. This led to types having more numerous driving wheels, such as the 2-6-0 Mogul, the 2-8-0 Consolidation, and, ultimately, the 2-10-2 Santa Fe.

Even larger locomotives were produced using the principle of articulation as typified by the Mallet Compound. This type was particularly favored on mountain railroads in the first decades of the twentieth century. In the 1920s, Superpower types were developed, with the heaviest freight locomotives being the 2-6-6-6 Alleghenies and the famous 520-ton 4-8-8-4 Big Boys.

These were perspectives never dreamed of in Britain and, although a move toward significantly bigger power occurred with the introduction of the L.M.S. Garratts in 1927, the 1930s saw continued building of inside-cylinder 0-6-0s and 2-8-0s. Only at the eleventh hour did the 2-10-0 appear, and few of these had a life of more than a few years owing to the witch-hunt to be rid of stream traction.

P.R.R. H CLASS
2-8-0

A Pennsylvania Railroad H-class Consolidation passes a signal tower with a long manifest freight in tow. During the course of more than 110 years of steam operations, the Pennsylvania Railroad operated more than 5,000 2-8-0 Consolidations on its lines. These comprised more than three dozen different classes and subclasses, all prefaced by the letter H, which P.R.R. used to designate the 2-8-0. In the latter years of steam operations, the most common classes of P.R.R. Consolidation were the H8, H9, and H10 classes, which featured many of the trademarks of twentieth-century P.R.R. steam power, including a large boiler and boxy Belpaire firebox. These weighed between 235,000 and 251,000 lbs and were well suited to moderate freight duties.

P.R.R. H CLASS
2-8-0

The 2-8-0 Consolidation was the most numerous of all steam locomotive types built for service in America. Often overshadowed by flashier types used in passenger service, Consolidations labored on ordinary freight trains all across the country for more than 80 years. In the days before dieselization, scenes such as this one of a Pennsylvania Railroad H-class 2-8-0 would have been considered ordinary to generations of passers-by.

P.R.R. H-CLASS NO. 108

2-8-0

Pennsylvania Railroad was among the first to adopt the 2-8-0 type. As early as 1864, the railroad was using a 2-8-0, albeit without a separate tender. Lehigh Valley began using 2-8-0s with separate tenders about 1868. At the time it was involved in a merger with another line, hence the common moniker of Consolidation for the 2-8-0 type. As one of the most common varieties of steam locomotives, the 2-8-0 Consolidation was primarily used as a heavy freight locomotive.

B.&O. CONSOLIDATION

2-8-0

The 2-8-0 Consolidation was a standard heavy freight locomotive in the latter part of the nineteenth century and in the early decades of the twentieth century. More 2-8-0s were built for service in North America than any other type of locomotive. With its four pairs of driving wheels, the Consolidation provided excellent adhesion and was well suited for moving long and heavy freights, especially in graded territory. Despite the advent of more powerful types, some railroads, such as the Baltimore & Ohio, continued to employ 2-8-0s in secondary freight service until the 1950s, when they were finally supplanted by modern diesel-electric locomotives.

B.&O. CONSOLIDATION NO. 2759

2-8-0

In the early 1950s, a Baltimore & Ohio 2-8-0 No. 2759 leads a coal drag into one of the railroad's many large freight yards. In its day, a Consolidation such as this Alco-built E-27 would have been wholly unremarkable and unworthy of a second glance from passing tourists. If one were to haul a coal train today, it would be an event not to be missed.

B.&O. CONSOLIDATION NO. 2810

2-8-0

Baltimore & Ohio ordered more than 600 Consolidations between 1902 and 1910, making them by far the most common type of steam locomotive on the line. Baltimore & Ohio No. 2810, pictured here in the early 1950s, was one of B.&O.'s most numerous varieties—its E-27 class. Alco built 414 of these 2-8-0s for B.&O. between 1905 and 1910, some of which survived as late as 1959.

B.&O. CONSOLIDATION NO. 2897

2-8-0

Baltimore & Ohio Consolidation No. 2897 is seen here leading a short freight at Grafton, West Virginia. The solid, powerful, and uncomplicated nature of the Consolidation contributed to its widespread popularity as America's number-one freight-hauling steam locomotive. Many locomotives had more impressive statistics than the basic 2-8-0, but more 2-8-0s were built in America than any other type. Although fewer were built after the introduction of the 2-8-2 Mikado, many vintage 2-8-0s had long and productive careers; some, such as B.&O. No. 2897, survived until the 1950s. Diesels changed the face of American railroading, and in a few years the entire scene had changed.

P.R.R. NO. 113

2-8-0

Size is relative: in the 1880s, the 2-8-0 Consolidation would have seemed huge compared with the 4-4-0s that were prevalent at the time. Yet the diminutive 2-8-0 of 1880 would have seemed small in comparison with one of P.R.R.'s heavy H9-class Consolidations of the 1910 period. By the mid-1920s, the H9 was dwarfed by P.R.R.'s massive I1 Decapods, and M1 Mountain types. Here an H-class Consolidation works with a manifest freight in the early 1950s, just a few years before it was replaced by diesels.

B.&O. MIKADOS IN COAL SERVICE

2-8-2

In the twentieth century, the 2-8-2 Mikado supplanted the 2-8-0 Consolidation as the most common type of locomotive ordered new for freight service. The long lifespan of a steam locomotive resulted in many lines operating Mikados and Consolidations together for decades. During the first half of the twentieth century, Baltimore & Ohio operated hundreds of both types working in coal and mixed freight service. Here a pair of B.&O. Mikados works a coal train. As some older bridges were not intended to support the great weight of these two engines, they were separated by a lone hopper for better weight distribution.

B.&O. MIKADO NO. 4547

2-8-2

Baltimore & Ohio Mikado No. 4547 marches into Grafton, West Virginia, with a mixed freight in tow. This Mikado is one of 100 class Q-3s built for the railroad by Baldwin in 1918. It was built to a United States Railroad Administration (U.S.R.A.) locomotive design—one of several moves intended to bring standardization to the American locomotive fleet. During the First World War, U.S.R.A. assumed operation of the privately owned American railroad network in an effort to coordinate operations and disentangle the quagmire caused by the onset of extraordinarily heavy wartime traffic. Efforts to standardize were largely waylaid when control of the railroads was returned to the private companies in the 1920s. Yet 30 years later, many U.S.R.A. locomotives were still hard at work.

DULUTH AND NORTHERN MIKADO

2-8-2

During the twentieth century, the 2-8-2 Mikado emerged as one of the most common types for general freight service in America. Thousands of Mikados worked freight services everywhere. Yet because they were so prolific, Mikados were too often ignored by photographers, who considered them ordinary and preferred more unusual subjects. This Baldwin-built Mikado worked for Duluth & Northern, Minnesota No. 14, and typifies the 2-8-2 of the First World War period.

NEW YORK CHICAGO & ST LOUIS H-5B CLASS

2-8-2

The New York Chicago & St Louis Railway was commonly known as the 'Nickel Plate Road'. Here, on August 14, 1947, one of its H-5b-class 2-8-2 Mikados poses at its yards in Conneaut, Ohio. This classic workhorse used a solid, well-balanced design. Built by Alco's Brooks Works in 1917, Nickel Plate Road No. 525 had served the railroad in freight service for three decades at the time of this photograph, and had another decade or so of service left before it was retired. By contrast, Nickel Plate Road's S-3-class 2-8-4 Berkshires, built in 1949 by Lima—and considered to be some of the finest of the type—were replaced by rather ordinary diesels with less than a decade's service behind them

CHESAPEAKE & OHIO K1 CLASS

2-8-2

On October 11, 1953, Chesapeake & Ohio K1-class 2-8-2 Mikado No. 1137 catches the sun at Rainelle, West Virginia. Although North American steam locomotives were largely utilitarian in design, each railroad adopted its own philosophy toward design and application of steam power. A railroad's mechanical officers worked with commercial builders in designing locomotives that would best suit a specific service. Every railroad had its own ideas for placement of external equipment such as headlights, bells, and sand domes. Some lines, such as New York Central, faced a restrictive loading gauge and needed to make their locomotives as compact as possible. Chesapeake & Ohio had its own considerations. Among its peculiarities was that it often situated air pumps at the front of the boiler, rather than the more common practice of hanging them from the side of the locomotive. The result did not have significant effects on operation, but greatly altered the locomotive's forward appearance.

P.R.R. MIKADOS

2-8-2

Pennsylvania Railroad's self-proclaimed moniker as the "Standard Railroad of the World" was frequently misinterpreted. Rather than setting standards for the rest of the industry, the Pennsylvania Railroad was the first American line to establish standard locomotive and equipment types with standardized spare parts on its own lines. For example, P.R.R. had 574 L1s-class Mikados. While these came from three different builders, each was built to the same design. Furthermore, except for the running gear, most of the primary components of the L1s were common with P.R.R.'s K4s-class Pacific, of which it had 425 examples. Here, in the mid-1950s, two of P.R.R.'s L1s's work nose to nose near Rockville, Pennsylvania.

P.R.R. DECAPOD

2-10-0

Characteristic of the trend toward larger, heavier, and substantially more powerful freight locomotives was Pennsylvania Railroad's development of its I1s-class Decapods. These exceptionally heavy locomotives featured 10 driving wheels—hence the name Decapod. The unusually large boiler and especially heavy appearance encouraged the I1s class to be known among railroaders as "Hippos". The first of the class was built in 1916 and, following roughly two years of testing, it entered regular production. Some were built at Pennsylvania Railroad's Juniata Shops in Altoona, Pennsylvania, while the majority were constructed commercially by the Baldwin Locomotive Works.

P.R.R. CLASS I1 DECAPOD

2-10-0

In the steam era, Pennsylvania Railroad was the leading mover of coal in America. In addition to heavy coal traffic, P.R.R. was a primary conduit for freight in the Northeast. In the 1920s, the railroad's Juniata shops developed the extremely powerful I1-class 2-10-0 Decapod for heavy freight service. Each of the I1 class was capable of doing the work of two H-class Consolidations, thus giving P.R.R. substantial savings by eliminating the necessity of the extra crew. Today, just one of these impressive machines remains.

SANTA FE NO. 979

2-10-2

Santa Fe Railway's 2-10-2 Santa Fe type No. 979 basks in the Californian sun at the railroad's shops in San Bernardino on October 26, 1947. It is believed that Santa Fe was the first railroad to adopt the 2-10-2 wheel arrangement, and so this arrangement is known as the Santa Fe type—regardless of the railroad that employed it. The first use of the 2-10-2 was on Raton Pass, where Santa Fe Railway adapted some 2-10-0 Decapods bought in 1902 with the addition of a rear trailing truck to improve tracking. Later 2-10-2s were built using the trailing truck to support a large firebox. In the First World War period, the 2-10-2 was adopted as a standard heavy freight locomotive.

SANTA FE RAILWAY MALLET COMPOUND

2-8-8-2

Santa Fe's 2-8-8-2 Mallet Compound No. 1791 was one of eight locomotives built by Alco in 1919 that the railroad acquired secondhand from Norfolk & Western. In the early decades of the twentieth century, the articulated Mallet Compound was a popular locomotive type for hauling very heavy freight. The Mallet is essentially two engines under a common boiler. Steam from the high-pressure cylinders (on the rear engine) is exhausted into the low-pressure cylinders on the forward engine.

L.M.S. 8F

2-8-0

Right from its formation in 1923, the L.M.S. struggled to equip itself with a modern heavy goods locomotive. Throughout the 1920s, it depended on ageing 0-8-0s and underpowered 0-6-0s to handle its considerable volume of freight traffic. Even the 33 Beyer-Garratts in 1927 had unredeemable faults, so it was only after the arrival of William Stanier in 1932 that the right locomotive for the job was born. Stanier's solution was an eight-coupled design derived from Churchward's G.W.R. 28XX class and incorporating the best features of the highly successful Black 5s.

L.M.S. GARRATT

2-6-6-2

For the first decade of its existence, Britain's L.M.S. suffered from the perpetuation of the Midland Railway's small-engine policy, resulting in the regular double-heading (operating two locomotives) of heavy freight trains by pairs of 0-6-0 tender engines. To remedy this, the management turned to Beyer Peacocks and ordered 33 Garratts, but unfortunately Midland thinking insisted that they had to be the equivalent of two 4F 0-6-0s in all their leading dimensions. They were inherently unsuited to fast running, due to poor valve events and typically Midland undersized bearings. As soon as the B.R. Standard 9Fs were in traffic, the Garratts were swiftly withdrawn.

L.M.S. 8F & 4F AT PEAK FOREST

2-8-0

In wartime Britain, the demand for heavy freight engines meant that Stanier 8Fs were built under government contracts by the G.W.R., L.N.E.R., and Southern workshops, and so were used on all the Big Four railways. Once Class 8 motive power became available for heavy freight haulage, the L.M.S. was able to reallocate its stock of 4F 0-6-0s to lesser duties. The changeover is captured perfectly by 8F No. 48605 bringing a lengthy rake of limestone empties through Peak Forest station, while the driver of 4F No. 43950 relaxes before taking out a local freight train.

P.R.R. ENGINE TERMINAL

High maintenance requirements leading to low locomotive availability and poor utilization were among steam locomotives' greatest failings. Railroads such as the Pennsylvania Railroad had thousands upon thousands of engines, which worked only a few hours a day on average. Furthermore, because locomotives were typically designed and built for very specialized service, it was common to find dozens of locomotives at major terminals awaiting serving or assignment. Diesels changed this scene very quickly—by 1958, they had supplanted steam on P.R.R.

P.R.R. J1 CLASS AND SANTA FE 5001 CLASS

2-10-4

Two of the best examples of the 2-10-4 Texas type ever built are pictured here. On the left is one of P.R.R.'s famous J1 class, a locomotive derived from Chesapeake & Ohio's T-1 Texas type. During the Second World War, P.R.R. was desperate for heavy freight power, and between 1942 and 1944 the railroad's Juniata Shops in Altoona, Pennsylvania, built 125 2-10-4s—the largest fleet of Texas types in America. On the right is one of Santa Fe Railway's ten 5001-class 2-10-4s. Built by Baldwin in 1938, they had 74-inch drive wheels and 30- x 34-inch cylinders—some of the largest ever employed by a simple engine and which are believed to have produced the greatest piston thrust of any American-built locomotive. In the mid-1950s, power-short P.R.R. borrowed some of Santa Fe's 2-10-4s to cover a surge of freight traffic.

NORFOLK & WESTERN
A CLASS

2-6-6-4

This is one of Norfolk & Western's famous A-class 2-6-6-4 simple articulated locomotives on March 6, 1953. N.&W.'s Roanoke Shops refined the high-speed simple articulated type to its highest level of perfection. The A class used roller-bearing-equipped lightweight drive-rods and other reciprocating parts, as well as precision counterbalancing to reduce the damaging effects of dynamic augment and improve the efficiency of the engine. This type was built from 1936 to 1950, and was operated in heavy freight service until 1959. Where N.&W. assigned its Y-class Mallet Compounds to heavy coal service in graded territory, the As were used more for fast manifest traffic and coal trains in more level territory.

UNION PACIFIC NO. 4023

4-8-8-4

Awed by the promise of Electro-Motive's new powerful four-unit FT diesel, Union Pacific worked with Alco in the design of a steam locomotive that could exceed the diesel's hauling ability. More to the point, Union Pacific wanted to eliminate the need for double-heading (operating two locomotives) heavy refrigerated box trains climbing east of Ogden, Utah, in the Wasatch Range. Thus the 4-8-8-4 Big Boy was born. Twenty-five of these massive locomotives were built between 1941 and 1944. Although they look ponderous, Big Boys were actually designed for speed, and could easily haul a heavy freight at 60 mph or faster. Frequently cited as the world's largest steam locomotive, the Big Boy was actually second to the 2-6-6-6 Allegheny. Here, Big Boy No. 4023 works Sherman Hill in central Wyoming.

NORFOLK & WESTERN
Y-6 CLASS

2-8-8-2

The Mallet Compound largely fell out of favor on American lines after the First World War. While articulated locomotives continued to be built, most were to simple designs where all cylinders received high-pressure steam directly from the boiler. An exception was at Norfolk & Western, which continued to refine and build Mallets until the end of steam. Its final and finest Mallets were the Y6bs. N.&W. Y6b No. 2200, built by Roanoke Shops in 1952, was the last steam locomotive built for heavy road service in America.

MIXED TRAFFIC

Mixed-traffic engine classes were a manifestation of the twentieth century and were brought about by two factors. First, freight trains had increased in speed and were approaching the speed of some passenger trains. Secondly, the trend to rationalize within motive-power fleets created the need for engines suitable for a wide range of duties. Such engines ultimately fulfilled most requirements on many of the world's railroads outside of the United States with the exception of the fastest trains and the heaviest of freight.

The genre, while not as widely recognized in the United States as in most parts of the world, did, however, find favor on branch lines. Branches tended to have more lightly built track that could not support the heaviest freight locomotives, and as a result intermediate types such as the 4-6-0 were often well suited to them. On many branches a single mixed train would carry both freight and passengers together.

After the First World War, railroads were under pressure from local trucking companies and looked to speed up their freight service to better compete. Fast freight trains demanded a whole new type of locomotive. By the late 1920s, a number of lines were ordering new 4-8-4s with moderately tall drivers that were sufficiently powerful for fast freight and fast enough for passenger services.

BALTIMORE & OHIO

2-8-0

Although largely a freight hauler, nothing actually prevented a 2-8-0 Consolidation from working in passenger service. Where passenger steam was characterized by tall drivers, the typical Consolidation would have had comparatively low drivers for high-tractive-effort applications at slower speeds. Yet, such a locomotive was well suited to a branch-line passenger train, where a requirement for lower axle weight and only nominal speeds was easily accommodated by a 2-8-0 such as this one pictured on the Baltimore & Ohio.

BOSTON & MAINE
4-4-0

The 4-4-0 is without question the most identifiable type of American locomotive and is known appropriately as the American type, or American standard. The success of the 4-4-0 resulted in its widespread production and application, as well as its exceptional longevity. Its simple, straightforward design, its three-point suspension, and its pair of driving wheels gave the locomotive flexibility, versatility, and power. Boston & Maine 4-4-0 No. 494 was built in 1892 by the Manchester Locomotive Works of Manchester, New Hampshire. With 66-inch driving wheels, this locomotive was largely used for passenger service and was typical of ordinary passenger locomotives of the period. Today, it is preserved at White River Junction, Vermont, as a static display next to the Amtrak passenger station.

CHINESE MIKADO
2-8-2

One of the earliest applications of the 2-8-2 type was exports built by the Baldwin Locomotive Works for Japan in 1897. At the time, Gilbert & Sullivan's opera *Mikado*—which depicted the Emperor of Japan—was enjoying popular performances, and so the new type became known as the Mikado. What was once exported from America was later imported to America—albeit from different places. The Boone & Scenic Valley's Chinese Mikado No. JS8419 pictured here—west of Boone, Iowa, in the summer of 1996—was built in China and was the last steam locomotive in the world built on a regular assembly line. It was sold to Iowa's Boone & Scenic Valley in 1988 and is used on the line's seasonal tourist trains.

K-36, 3'-GAUGE MIKADO
2-8-2

The Baldwin Locomotive Works was the largest supplier of narrow-gauge steam locomotives in America. Among the most modern narrow-gauge designs were several classes of unusually heavy three-foot-gauge 2-8-2 Mikados for the Denver & Rio Grande Western. Unlike standard-gauge locomotives, these featured outside frames, outside crankpins and counterweights instead of conventional running gear and counterweights. This arrangement immediately distinguishes Rio Grande's three-foot-gauge Mikados from all other types.

AMERICAN NO. 436
4-4-0

Choice of fuel had a distinct influence on locomotive design. The most common fuel in America was bituminous coal. However, railroads serving the anthracite-producing region of eastern Pennsylvania, often bought locomotives designed to burn this fuel. Anthracite burners required a firebox with a larger grate area to accommodate a slower, hotter burn quality. Many such locomotives used the Wootton firebox, which was so broad it made a conventional cab design impractical. To solve this problem, the Camelback locomotive was developed with a split cab, with the engineer riding in the forward cab and the fireman riding on a small platform at the back. Delaware & Hudson's 4-4-0 American No. 436 is of this design. The locomotive was not superheated; instead of modern piston valves that use a cylindrical shape above the cylinders, it has the more traditional boxy D-style slide valves.

NORTHERN PACIFIC
NO. 328
4-6-0

The Ten-Wheeler was not a modern arrangement and was first used in the 1840s. The arrangement gained in popularity in the 1860s as a passenger locomotive and was built with ever larger dimensions into the early twentieth century for both freight and passenger applications. Northern Pacific No. 328 was built at the Rogers works of the American Locomotive Company in 1905 and is a fairly typical example of an early twentieth-century 4-6-0.

NORTHERN PACIFIC
NO. 328
4-6-0

Using three pairs of driving wheels and a nominally larger boiler, the 4-6-0 Ten-Wheeler type provided greater power and traction than the typical 4-4-0 American type it supplanted. By the turn of the twentieth century, American railroads were moving significantly heavier and longer trains. Yet the evolution of types moved rapidly, and the 4-6-0s were soon bumped to secondary and branch-line services by even larger machines. Some 4-6-0s continued to labor on rural branch lines until the end of steam in the late 1950s. Northern Pacific No. 328 survived long past its mainline service.

STRASBURG RAILROAD
4-8-0

Strasburg Railroad No. 475 is a former Norfolk & Western 4-8-0 Mastodon type. First developed by the Lehigh Valley after the Civil War, the 4-8-0 Mastodon was an uncommon type in America. Locomotive historian Alfred W. Bruce estimated that just 580 4-8-0s were built for domestic service. Most lines preferred either 2-8-0 Consolidations (also developed by the Lehigh Valley) for freight work, or 4-6-0s for passenger work or dual services. Only six American 4-8-0s were saved from scrapping, making it one of the most unusual preserved types. This one serves on the Strasburg Railroad—a successful tourist line in eastern Pennsylvania.

EAST BROAD TOP NO. 14
2-8-2

East Broad Top purchased six Baldwin-built Mikados between 1911 and 1920, to replace older 2-8-0 Consolidations in coal-hauling service. Although built for three-foot-gauge track, these are fairly traditional locomotives. Unlike Rio Grande's three-foot-gauge Mikados, E.B.T.'s Mikados use a conventional inside-frame arrangement. Here, East Broad Top No. 14 makes a nice show at Orbisonia, Pennsylvania, in October 1997.

L.N.E.R. K1

2-6-0

In Britain, the 1945 rebuilding of Gresley's three-cylinder Mogul "MacCailin Mor" with two cylinders was overseen by Arthur Peppercorn. When Peppercorn succeeded Edward Thompson, he made the engine the prototype for this useful and versatile mixed-traffic class. Although an L.N.E.R. design, they were all delivered after nationalization as B.R. Nos 62001–70. They worked extensively over the northeastern region of England and on the West Highland line in Scotland, but dieselization cut short their working lives and only one engine, No. 62005, survives in preservation.

SOUTHERN PACIFIC
NO. 3686

2-10-2

Southern Pacific faced mountain grades everywhere it went ,and so to conquer them it operated hundreds of powerful and very impressive locomotives. Long trains were frequently assigned helpers at the bases of grades. In this March 1951 view, a Southern Pacific 2-10-2 No. 3686 and a 4-8-4 lead train No. 20 are at milepost 323 near Shasta Springs, on the grade between Dunsmuir and Grass Lake, California. The 2-10-2 was a standard heavy freight locomotive on Southern Pacific, and its 10 coupled drivers gave it great pulling power to overcome steep gradients.

S.R. U

2-6-0

In Britain, in August 1927, the disastrous Sevenoaks derailment of one of Richard Maunsell's K-class express 2-6-4Ts caused 20 planned additional locomotives to be built instead as 2-6-0 tender engines. Simultaneously, the 20 K-class tanks were rebuilt as Moguls and incorporated into the new U class. Eventually numbering 50 engines, the U class, with their six-foot (1.9 m) driving wheels, were employed throughout the Southern system. They were considered by engineers to be the best of Maunsell's Moguls for passenger work and were noted for their exploits west of Exeter and on the Reading–Redhill line.

L.M.S. BLACK 5

4-6-0

The free-steaming qualities of the Class 5's boiler, combined with William Stanier's careful attention to the valve events, comfortably allowed speeds of up to 90 mph. Besides the 75 engines originally ordered, the L.M.S. was responsible for the largest single locomotive building contract placed by a British railwroad company, when a further 227 engines were ordered from Armstrong Whitworth on Tyneside. By the end of 1938, there were 472 Class 5s at work. Construction resumed in 1943, and thereafter the workshops at Crewe, Derby, and Horwich turned out batches every year until 1951, until no fewer than 842 engines were in traffic.

L.M.S. BLACK 5 NO. 44932

4-6-0

Prompted by the success of the G.W.R. Hall-class 4-6-0s, William Stanier gave the design of a similar general-purpose locomotive top priority on joining the L.M.S. from Swindon in 1932. It was just the type of standard locomotive that the railroad needed to replace a mixed bag of ageing pre-grouping classes. So great was the need that the first orders were placed straight off the drawing board, with Crewe works and Vulcan Foundry sharing the load. The size and weight of the Class 5 gave it virtually unrestricted access to the entire L.M.S. system. It could be used on almost any duty, from dealing with loose-coupled freight trains to express passenger services.

L.M.S. BLACK 5 NO. 45428
4-6-0

As well as exhibiting variations in valve gear and exhaust arrangements, the postwar British L.M.S. Black 5s incorporated devices that were to become obligatory on the B.R. Standard designs: self-cleaning smokeboxes, rocking grates, and self-emptying ashpans. And, of course, the Black 5 itself became the basis for Robert Riddles' B.R. 5MT 4-6-0, totaling another 172 locomotives, which are the obvious descendants of the L.M.S. engines.

GOLDEN ARROW
BULLEID LIGHT PACIFIC

When new, Britain's S.R. Bulleid Pacifics bristled with novel features. The "air-smoothed" casing was intended to be cleaned by passing through the coach-washing plant, rather than being an attempt at streamlining. The "boxpok" wheel centers saved over a third of the weight of conventional wheels. The magnificent 280 lb boiler contained an all-welded steel firebox fitted with thermic syphons, to improve water circulation. There was a Lemaitre multiple-jet blastpipe, rocking firegrate, electric lighting, and, of course, the innovative chain-driven valve gear. To give it even more visual impact, the locomotive was finished in bright malachite-green paintwork with broad yellow stripes.

S.R. BULLEID REBUILT LIGHT PACIFIC

By 1957 in Britain, the level of maintenance demanded by such problematic mechanisms as chain-driven valve gear could not be justified, and a scheme was drawn up to rebuild 60 of the Bulleid Light Pacifics along the same lines as the Merchant Navies. The fundamental changes were the substitution of Walschaerts valve gear and the removal of the air-smoothed casing. Thus rejuvenated, the rebuilt engines put in fine performances right up to the last day of Southern steam in July 1967. Remarkably, no fewer than 20 of the type have passed into preservation, nine of them in unrebuilt condition.

UNION PACIFIC NO. 844

4-8-4

Following years of mergers, consolidation, and line abandonment, one of the last traditional railroad companies left operating in America is Union Pacific. It was chartered in the 1860s to build the eastern section of the first Transcontinental Railroad. Today, Union Pacific is the last remaining traditional railroad to operate steam locomotives that were built new for the company. Northern type No. 844 was the railroad's last new steam locomotive, built in 1944 by Alco. On occasion, between excursion assignments, No. 844 is operated in freight service by Union Pacific, such as the one seen in this 1989 view at Grand Island, Nebraska.

UNION PACIFIC NO. 844

4-8-4

Union Pacific's last new steam locomotive was No. 844, built by Alco in 1944. This magnificent 4-8-4 Northern was never retired and has remained on the roster until the present day. Although primarily retained for passenger excursions, it has occasionally worked in freight service as well, as seen here in another view near Grand Island, Nebraska, in September 1996.

FAIRBURN 42095 WITH IVATT 2MT IN BACKGROUND

2-6-4T

In a shed scene redolent of the last days of steam on British Railways, the motive-power allocation is dominated by postwar L.M.S. designs. No. 42095 is one of the 277 Fairburn 4MT 2-6-4 tanks built in 1945 as a shorter-wheelbase development of William Stanier's pre-war design. No. 46514 is one of the 25 Ivatt 2MT 2-6-0s whose modern labour-saving features and "go anywhere" usefulness endeared them to crews and shed staff alike. An 8F and a Black 5 complete the scene.

B1 MAYFLOWER SILHOUETTE

4-6-0

One of the two preserved L.N.E.R. Thompson B1 4-6-0s, No. 1306 *Mayflower*, embodies the romance of the steam railroad as it is silhouetted against the sunset at the head of a late-afternoon train on the Great Central Railway. For many years while the former G.C.R. mainline was under B.R. Eastern Region control, the B1s were regularly seen on all classes of train, heading north from London Marylebone bound for Leicester, Nottingham, and Sheffield.

S.R. WEST COUNTRY

4-6-2

Essentially a scaled-down version of S.R. Bulleid's Merchant Navy class of 1941, the first of his Light Pacifics emerged from Brighton works in May 1945. The class was rapidly multiplied until no fewer than 110 were in service, most being named after locations in the west of England, but 44 locomotives were named after aircraft, airfields, RAF squadrons, and personalities associated with the Second Wrold War's Battle of Britain. The Light Pacifics shared many of the design features of the bigger Merchant Navies, but the principal differences were aimed at saving weight, to allow them to operate almost anywhere on the Southern system.

SOUTHERN PACIFIC NO. 4449

4-8-4

Southern Pacific was the largest passenger carrier in the American West. When ridership and revenues went into steep decline in the 1930s, S.P. made a bold move to boost ridership by introducing its now famous *Daylight* streamlined passenger trains between San Francisco and Los Angeles. Later, S.P. expanded the *Daylight* to include a whole family of streamliners. S.P.'s GS-4-class 4-8-4s were built as general-service locomotives in 1941, but streamlined and styled for *Daylight* services. These augmented GS-2s and GS-3 4-8-4s built earlier for *Daylight* service. S.P. GS-4 No. 4449, built in 1949, was preserved. In the 1980s, it was restored to service and operates occasional excursions, such as this one en route to Sacramento seen at Brock, California, in 1991.

B.R. STANDARD 4MT

2-6-4T

Although designed at Brighton works, the handsome B.R. Standard Class 4MT tanks owed their pedigree to the Stanier and Fairburn tanks of the L.M.S. One hundred and fifty-five examples were built, mostly at Brighton, and their brisk acceleration and lively turn of speed made them ideal for hauling tightly timed commuter services, as they proved on the London, Tilbury, and Southend line and on the Glasgow suburbans. Their versatility made them popular engines with the crews, and no fewer than eight have survived in preservation.

Branch-Line & Suburban Locomotives

Despite the lighter track of branch lines, in 1850 there would have been little difference between branch-line and mainline locomotives. Early suburban steam trains were worked by the celebrated Forney 0-4-4s on the elevated railroads of New York and Chicago, but the noise and smoke in city environments meant that these lines were electrified in the early twentieth century. Tank engines were used on suburban services by such railroads as the New York Central, Central Railroad of New Jersey, Illinois Central, and Boston and Albany.

By 1910, the difference in size and weight was profound and, as few railroads were keen to invest in specifically designed branch-line locomotives, older locomotives were often reassigned to branch-line work. As a result, venerable 4-4-0s and 2-6-0s built in the 1870s and 1880s worked American branch lines until the 1930s; as 2-8-2s, 2-8-4s, and other modern machines claimed the bulk of mainline freight, 4-6-0s and 2-8-0s were also cascaded into branch-line work.

A similar system occurred in Britain, although in addition certain definitive switching types, such as the Great Western 5700 and L.M.S. Jinty, did work passenger trains on secondary and branch lines. The situation became fully clarified with the British Railways Standard designs which covered a wide range of mixed-traffic types suitable for every level of service throughout the network.

BERKELEY RAILROAD
FORNEY
0-4-4-T

Although useful for short-range slow-speed switching operations, tank engines of the mid-nineteenth century were not suited for most operations because, as they traveled, the change in weight resulting from the depletion of fuel and water reserves lowered the adhesive weight of the engine. To solve this problem, Matthias Forney patented this unusual type of tank engine in 1866, which was intended to minimize changes to tractive effort (and thus pulling capacity) as the fuel and water were used up. Its short wheelbase and relatively light axle load made it ideal for sharp curves and lightly built bridges.

FESTINIOG RAILWAY
DOUBLE-FAIRLIE
0-6-0+0-6-0

The rapid growth of slate traffic on the Festiniog Railway in Wales soon called for something stronger than its small George England 0-4-0Ts of 1863. The answer was a "double engine" a design patented by Robert Fairlie. In this, a twin boiler unit sharing a central firebox was mounted on the mainframe supported on two power trucks. The engineer and fireman occupied a central cab, with one man on either side of the firebox. Four engines were built between 1869 and 1885, the last pair being constructed at the company's Boston Lodge works.

ISLE OF MAN BEYER PEACOCK

2-4-0T

The design of these charming little engines was derived from very similar 3'6"-gauge machines that the English manufacturer Beyer Peacock supplied to the Norwegian State Railway in 1871. The Manx engines were developed in four distinct stages over a period of half a century, each subsequent batch being of larger capacity to cope with the ever-increasing volume of traffic on the island's railroads. An identical locomotive supplied to the Manx Northern Railway in 1880 was later acquired by the I.M.R. as its No. 14 *Thornhill*, while two others of the same design were built for the Ballymena & Larne Railway in Ireland.

NORTH LONDON RAILWAY 75

0-6-0T

J.C. Park introduced his 75-class short-wheelbase 0-6-0Ts in 1879, to negotiate the tightly curved sidings in London's Docklands. They were remarkably powerful machines and continued to work at Poplar docks until the mid-1950s. However, back in 1931, the L.M.S. had sent two to work on the Cromford & High Peak line in Derbyshire, where their short wheelbase and abundant power made them ideally suited to the fearsome C.&H.P. gradients, and further engines were relocated from London. In 1960, the last survivor, No. 58850, was saved for preservation on the Bluebell Railway.

L.S.W.R. ADAMS RADIAL TANKS

4-4-2T

In Britain William Adams advocated using a leading truck in his locomotives, and his first design was a 4-4-0 suburban tank, soon extended to a 4-4-2T. The 59 engines of his 415 class of 1882 successfully developed this theme, but their time hauling London commuters was comparatively brief. Withdrawals began in 1916, and all had gone by the mid-1920s except two retained for working the tortuous Lyme Regis branch in Dorset. A third was bought back from Colonel Stephens's East Kent Railway, and the trio worked the branch until 1961. Ex-E.K.R. No. 488 was saved for preservation by the Bluebell Railway.

L.N.W.R. COAL TANK
0-6-2T

Under F.W. Webb, Crewe works became synonymous with ruthless cost control, standardization, and mass production of a family of austere and dignified locomotives. Webb's Coal Tanks of 1881 were strong and workmanlike, and, despite their name, were widely used on passenger as well as freight work. Three hundred examples were built over a period of 17, years and their capacity for hard work left more than 60 in traffic at nationalization, distributed across the former L.N.W.R. system between Lancashire and South Wales. The last Coal Tank retired as B.R. No. 58926 in 1958 and was saved for posterity.

L.S.W.R. O2
0-4-4T

William Adams's medium-sized O2 suburban tanks were introduced in 1889, but after only a decade were displaced from many of their duties by Drummond's much larger M7 class. However, their modest size and lively acceleration made them ideal candidates to revitalize the Isle of Wight services and 21 were shipped across by the Southern Railway. Fitted with Westinghouse brakes and extended bunkers, and carrying island names, the O2s lasted in service until the end of Isle of Wight steam in 1966. No. W24 *Calbourne* was saved for preservation on the Isle of Wight Steam Railway.

C.R. NO. 55195 AT KILLIN

0-4-4T

The engineering legacy of Britain's Dugald Drummond endured on the Caledonian Railway in Scotland long after his departure. Drummond himself was much influenced by his mentor, William Stroudley, and it is easy to see both men's design hallmarks of rounded tank tops, leading splasher sandboxes, and elegant but narrow cabs in the family of 0-4-4 tanks produced by his successors at St. Rollox works. John Lambie's 19 class of 1895 was quickly followed by the more numerous but virtually identical McIntosh 439 class of 1900. William Pickersgill added his own version of the latter class ,and there was even a batch of 10 built by the L.M.S. in 1925.

COLORADO & SOUTHERN NARROW-GAUGE NO. 70

2-8-0

On September 15, 1937, a Colorado & Southern 2-8-0 Consolidation leads a freight at Georgetown, Colorado, on its ascent of the Front Range. C.&S. was a Burlington affiliate and, like Denver & Rio Grande Western, operated a three-foot network in Colorado. Built by Baldwin in 1897, in most respects No. 70 is a scaled-down standard-gauge 2-8-0. Among its unusual features as pictured here are the two air-reservoir cylinders located atop the boiler.

S.E.&C.R. H & M7

0-4-4T

Most of the major railroad companies running suburban services into the London terminals adopted the 0-4-4T, as it gave the opportunity to fit a reasonable-sized boiler on a truck chassis, giving good riding qualities when running in reverse. For the S.E.&C.R. commuter trains into London's Charing Cross, Harry Wainwright provided his pretty H class, while over at Waterloo, Dugald Drummond's somewhat larger M7s were in charge. Suburban electrification displaced both types onto rural and secondary duties, and more than a third of each class were fitted for push-pull working. Nearly all were retained as reliable branch-line engines by British Railways, resulting in examples of both classes surviving in active preservation.

W.&L.L.R.

0-6-0T

These compact and sturdy little engines built by British manufacturer Beyer Peacock for the opening of the 2'6"-gauge Welshpool & Llanfair Light Railway in Wales are still at work on the line today. the *Earl* and the *Countess*, named in honor of the Earl and Countess of Powys, handled all the traffic on the steeply graded line from its opening in 1903 to closure in 1956. Although somewhat "Great Westernized" in appearance, they retain many of their classic Gorton features. When the line was closed by British Railways, both locomotives were taken to Oswestry works, returning to Llanfair in triumph when the railway reopened in 1963.

KETTLE MORAINE RAILWAY PRAIRIE

2-6-2

The 2-6-2 Prairie never enjoyed the widespread acceptance of the 4-6-2 Pacific or the 2-8-0 Consolidation. Some 1,700 were built, and it was most popular with railroads in the American Midwest, hence its name. While in the first decade of the twentieth century it was briefly built for both mainline freight and passenger service, the Prairie soon proved more suitable for branch-line use. Kettle Moraine Railway No. 9 was the latter variety of Prairie. It was built by Baldwin in 1901 for California's McCloud River Railroad. After more than 60 years of working for a variety of small Western lines, it was preserved in Wisconsin.

SAGINAW TIMBER NO. 2

2-8-2

Many railroads from the First World War period until the end of steam operations assigned 2-8-2 Mikados to general freight work. Saginaw Timber No. 2 is a relatively lightweight Mikado-type locomotive typical of the type that served rural branch lines and short-line railways. The locomotive shown here worked in tourist train service during the 1990s and is one of several locomotives preserved at the Mid-Continent Railway Museum at North Freedom, Wisconsin.

G.W.R. 57XX

0-6-0PT

Equally at home hauling branch-line passenger trains, in later years a handful of the numerous 57XX panniers ventured away from the Western Region, undertaking banking work on the Folkestone Harbour incline and pilot duties at London's Waterloo. Some surplus engines were sold to the National Coal Board and, in 1956, London Transport began acquiring them to replace former Metropolitan Railway locomotives on switching work and engineers' trains. A total of 14 pannier tanks saw L.T. service, and three of these remained at work until 1971. This trio now numbers among the 16 survivors that continue to prove their worth in preservation.

G.W.R. 61XX

2-6-2T

There were several G.W.R. classes of large 2-6-2T built for suburban passenger work, the 61XX class of 1931 being the final development and most powerful of its type. For many years, the whole class of 70 engines worked entirely in the London division, the vast majority from Southall, Slough, and Old Oak Common sheds. Introduced to replace ageing 4-4-2 and 2-4-0 tanks, the 61XX class proved highly successful, and several of the class survived until the last day of steam traction on the Western Region.

L.M.S. 2MT

2-6-2T

On the Southern Region, Ivatt's handsome little Class 2 2-6-2Ts were the most modern passenger tanks available and displaced elderly pre-Grouping engines, often being rostered for duties intended for more powerful locomotives. It was the S.R.'s engines which lasted in service the longest (until 1967), and four of these have survived in preservation. Two have been restored to working order: No. 41241 on the Keighley & Worth Valley Railway in West Yorkshire and No. 41312 on the Mid-Hants Railway in Hampshire.

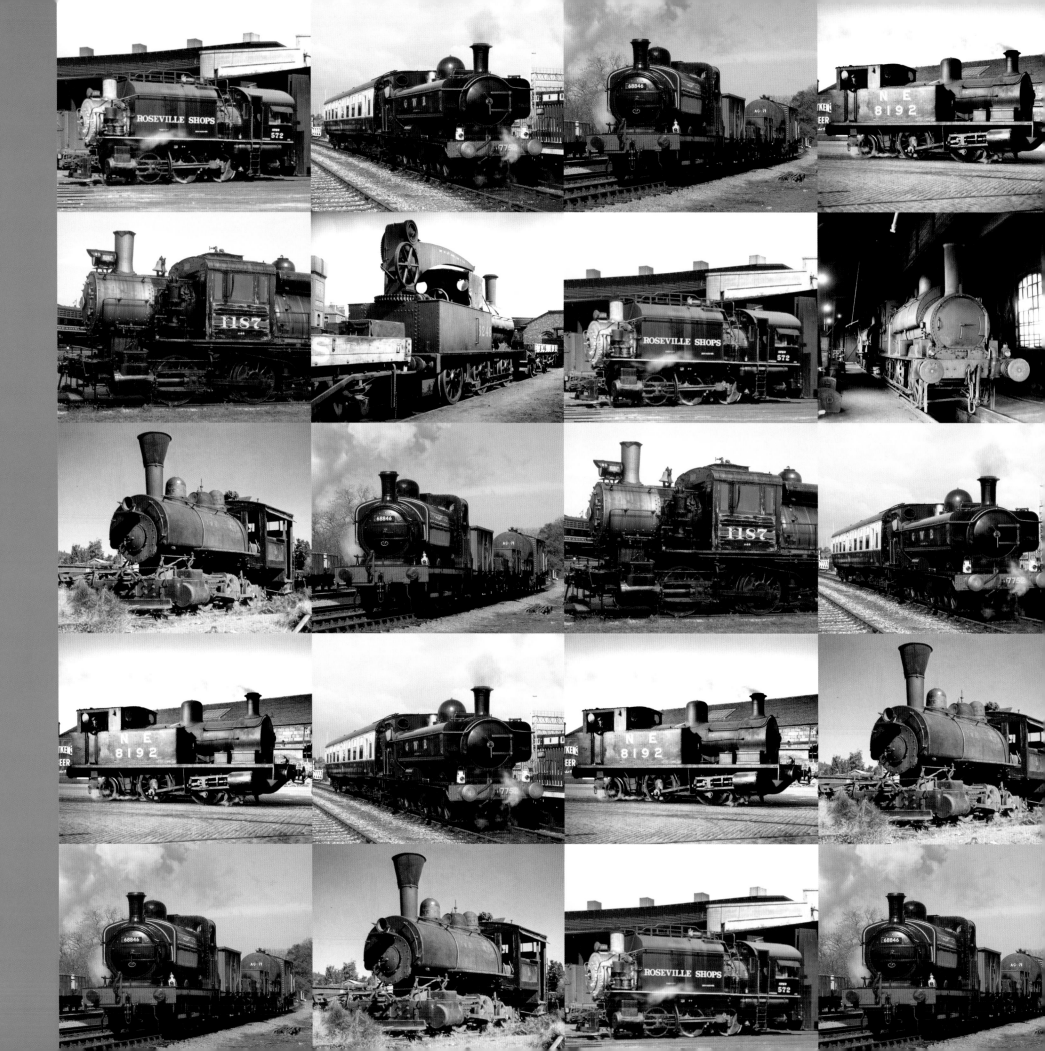

SWITCHERS

As the railroads became unified, huge marshaling yards developed at important junctions, where wagons had to be switched into new consists in order to reach their various destinations. The locomotives for this work were designed for maximum adhesion and easy maneuvrability and were all across America. They could be found drilling the yards, working large passenger terminals, and switching freight cars on sidings served by mainlines. The most common types were 0-4-0s and 0-6-0s. These placed the full adhesive weight of the locomotive on driving wheels and did not require pilot wheels because they rarely needed to travel more than about 20 mph.

Although thousands of steam switchers were built, very few were ordered new after 1930. Often railroads dieselized switching operations early to take advantage of great savings afforded by diesel switchers, which required less servicing, enjoyed higher availability, and benefitted from superior starting characteristics. Diesels were also preferred in places where smoke ordinances discouraged the use of steam.

In Britain, 0-6-0 switchers were also prevalent in the form of tank engines, although, by the 1930s, the first British diesels appeared in the marshaling yards. Many downgraded ex-mainline inside-cylinder 0-6-0s also eked out their days in switching operations and, as in America, the development of switching locomotives effectively ceased by 1930.

ROSEVILLE SHOPS SWITCHER

0-6-0T

Each of Southern Pacific's major locomotive shops employed a specially designed 0-6-0T tank switcher for moving locomotives and tenders within the shop complex. Instead of a tender, an 0-6-0T stored water on a saddle-type tank mounted over the boiler. This had the added advantage of using the boiler water as ballast to improve traction. Although not pretty to look at, and not as often photographed as the big mainline locomotives, shop switchers were often mascots of shopmen, who treated the locomotives with extra attention and a degree of affection.

TANK ENGINE

0-6-0

Tank engines such as this one were ideal for industrial switching. They placed the full weight of the engine on driving wheels, and, as they had a short wheelbase and carried engine water in a tank rather than a trailing tender, they could easily negotiate tight curvature and travel in either direction with relative ease. These small locomotives were often operated on industrial lines for years after the conclusion of mainline steam.

NORTH LONDON RAILWAY CRANE TANK

0-4-2

This engine started life in 1858 as a small 0-4-0ST built by Sharp Stewart & Co. for working between Hammersmith and Acton in London. It was taken over by the N.L.R. shortly afterward and rebuilt in 1872 with an additional trailing axle supporting a crane, and in this form it spent the next 80 years of its life as works switcher at Bow. It became the oldest engine inherited by British Railways at nationalization, and there were hopes that it would achieve its working centenary. But alas, the little crane tank was withdrawn in 1951 and sent to Derby, where it remained for several months before being scrapped.

L.N.W.R. RAMSBOTTOM SPECIAL TANKS

0-6-0ST

This long-lived class of 0-6-0STs was built at Crewe in considerable numbers from 1870 onward and was the standard switching engine for many years throughout the L.N.W.R. Indeed, five of them continued in departmental service until after nationalization of Britain's railroads, with the last survivors switching at Wolverton Carriage Works until 1959. Six examples were built with slightly larger driving wheels to 5'3" gauge between 1873 and 1898, for use on the L.N.W.R.'s Irish offshoot, the Dundalk, Newry & Greenore Railway. These hauled all the traffic on the line until 1933, and the last survivors remained in action until 1952. To the end, they retained their old L.N.W.R. livery and characteristics.

L.N.W.R. CRANE TANK NOS. 3247 & 3248

0-4-2

For moving heavy materials as well as performing general switching duties around a locomotive works yard, a crane tank locomotive is an indispensable piece of railroad equipment, so F.W. Webb designed a pair of 0-4-2 saddle tanks for duties at Crewe in 1892. These useful machines had their crane mounted at the rear of the coal bunker; however, to permit them to travel out onto the running lines of the L.N.W.R., the crane jib could not be raised, but could, of course, slew through 360 degrees. These crane tanks had long and useful lives, the last being withdrawn in 1946.

G.N.R. J52

0-6-0ST

For almost a century, the G.N.R. and its successors relied on six-coupled saddle tanks for switching and local freight work. The final development of the type came in 1897, when Henry Ivatt introduced his J13 class, an enlarged version of earlier Stirling engines. Further examples came from outside builders until 1909, when the class numbered 85 engines. Apart from switching the freight yards in London and alongside the East Coast mainline, they were employed on transfer freights across the capital, duties that were inevitably taken over by diesel switchers, and large numbers were retired in the late 1950s. No. 1247 was bought for preservation by Captain Bill Smith in 1959.

READING COMPANY CAMELBACK

0-4-0

One of the most common wheel arrangements used for switchers on American lines was the basic 0-4-0. The combination of full adhesive weight on drivers with a short wheelbase made this arrangement ideal for working industrial and yard trackage with tight curvature. This Reading Company 0-4-0 is unusual because it features the Camelback arrangement, where the engineer's cab straddles the boiler, while the fireman's platform and cab remain at the rear. This was necessitated by the application of a Wootten firebox, which featured an unusually large grate for burning anthracite coal. Many of the anthracite-hauling lines, including the Reading, Lackawanna, Central Railroad of New Jersey, and Erie Railroad, employed Camelback types. More common than Camelback 0-4-0s were road types such as 4-6-0s, 4-4-2s, and 2-8-0s. Difficulties in communication between firemen and engineers made camelbacks unpopular, and very few were built after 1915. This one is preserved in static condition at Strasburg, Pennsylvania.

BALDWIN

0-10-0

The 0-10-0 type was an extreme variation of the switcher developed specifically for heavy yard work in the early years of the twentieth century. With 10 driving wheels placing the full adhesive weight of the locomotive on the rail, the 0-10-0 was capable of enormous tractive effort, but not great speed. It was often used in hump yards to shove long strings of freight cars for sorting.

GREAT NORTH OF SCOTLAND RAILWAY Z5

0-4-2T

Two of these engines were supplied by Manning Wardle & Co. for the inauguration of locomotive haulage on the Aberdeen Harbour lines in 1915. They were neat little outside-cylindered side tanks, but on arrival were found to be two tonnes heavier than specified. Two slightly smaller versions (Z4 Class) were ordered from the same makers, but the heavier engines were retained, and all four spent their working lives in Aberdeen docks. Both classes retained their pre-grouping livery until 1939, therafter becoming plain black under L.N.E.R. and B.R. ownership.

G.W.R. 57XX

0-6-0PT

Distinct from other British mainline railroads, the Great Western preferred to equip its tank engines with pannier tanks slung either side of the boiler. Thanks to the wealth of small tank engines already owned by the G.W.R. when the first pannier tanks appeared in 1898, Churchward saw no need for large-scale construction. Many of the early locomotives were worn out by 1929, however, so Collett introduced the 57XX class as an enlarged and improved version of Churchward's engines. Swindon works and outside builders constructed a massive total of 863 locomotives over the next 17 years. They were equally at home on switching work, local freight trains, handling empty coaching stock, or on branch lines.

OVERSEAS EXPORTS

Britain, as railroad builder to an empire and the world, assumed supremacy in locomotive production and, in the early days at least, what was good for Britain was good for the rest of the world, too. Engines whose spiritual home was to be found in the soft English countryside could be seen active on all continents. Tens of thousands of locomotives were built by foundries the names of which now enshrined in industrial legend. The engines were rolled on to the decks of ships to pioneer Britain's Industrial Revolution across the world.

British supremacy was challenged at the beginning of the twentieth century, when, having equipped the home roads, the big American builders began an aggressive export drive. In some ways, the rugged simplicity of the American exports proved ideal in the rough and tumble of the world at large. Many were of a mixed-traffic concept, and their bar frames proved tougher than the traditional British plate frames when working on indifferent track beds; their wide fireboxes proved superior for burning variable qualities of coal, while easy maintenance and access to working parts were ever welcome.

In terms of world locomotive distribution, British and American were the two principal schools, and railroads in many countries employed examples of each.

5'6"-GAUGE IN CHILE
4-6-0

This high-stepping chocolate-colored 10-wheeled beauty was the works pilot at San Bernardo Works in the Chilean capital Santiago. The 5'6"-gauge veteran was the last survivor of the once numerous Chilean State Railway's 38 class. She was also believed to be the last surviving engine built by Rogers of New Jersey, having come from its works in 1896. Rogers was responsible for many stylish engines prior to its absorption into Alco in 1905.

INDIAN RAILWAYS SGC2/XC

Two classic Indian locomotive types for the subcontinent's 5'6"-gauge mainlines are shown here. The inside cylinder 0-6-0 on the left was one of a type originally introduced by the B.E.S.A. standardization program of 1903 and was built by the Vulcan Foundry at Newton le Willows, Lancashire, England, for the East Indian Railway in 1913. The handsome XC class Pacific on the right, built in 1928, also by the Vulcan Foundry, was one of the famous X Series Standards of the 1920s. The XCs were the last large British express passenger engines left in world service and survived in Bengal until the 1980s. None has been preserved.

BALDWIN FIRELESS, CUBA

0-4-0

The concept of a steam locomotive without a fire is unimaginable to most people, but the Fireless is ideal for switching in works or factories which have a ready supply of high-pressure steam. Steam and boiling water are injected at high pressure into a storage vessel on the engine and fed to the cylinders via a reducing valve, in order to achieve a constant power output. The Fireless was an efficient and economical switcher; there was nothing to go wrong and only a driver was needed. This example, photographed at Bolivia Sugar Mill in Camaguey province, Cuba, on April 21, 1988, was built by Baldwin in 1917.

PORTER MOGUL, CUBA

2-6-0

Cuba holds the world's last bastion of classic American steam ,and some of the island's locomotive roster are actually former American-railroad locomotives. Frozen in time by Fidel Castro's 1959 revolution, a huge variety of different types exist with few more recent than 1920 and some examples dating back to the 1870s. Dozens of different classes make up the island's roster. A range of different gauges is also in operation and, combined with the different liveries applied by the various mills, variety is of the essence. Here, at the Carlos Manuel de Cespedes Mill in Camaguey province, a Mogul, built by Porter in 1919, draws a caboose into the factory yard on April 20, 1988.

THE BALDWIN DRAGON

0-6-0

One of the most delightful enclaves of American industrial locomotives was Negros island in the Philippines, which was home to the Dragons of the Hawaiian Philippine Company. The company had a stud of six Baldwin 0-6-0s, built between 1919 and 1928, along with a pair of Baldwin 0-6-2STs which originated on the company's plantations on Hawaii. Here is Dragon No. 6, fitted with a stovepipe smokestack following conversion to oil burning. Usually these engines burn bagasse, the natural waste product of the sugarcane-crushing process, and it is this straw-like substance which gives rise to the heavy emissions of fire—hence the official designation 'Dragons'.

VULCAN IRON WORKS

0-6-0

The tropical island of Java in Indonesia now holds the world's most active steam roster on its sugar plantations. In common with Cuba, Java's sugar industry has declined; many mills have closed, while trucking of cane has also been a factor in running down the railroad network. As Cuba is the last haven of American steam power, so is Java for European, with many different designs having come from German and Dutch builders—Java once being part of the Dutch East Indies. Virtually no American—or, for that matter, British—engines can be found on Java. One exception is this sprightly 0-6-0, seen at Jatiwangi Sugar Mill in July 1989. The engine was built by Vulcan Iron Works in 1920.

INDIAN CONTRASTS

2-8-0 and 4-6-2

Two leading schools of locomotive design are seen here at Jamalpur Motive Power Depot in Bengal, India. On the left is a HGS-Class heavy freight 2-8-0, built by the North British of Glasgow in 1920 for the East India Railway, while on the right, in absolute contrast, is an express passenger-hauling WP Pacific, built by Baldwin in 1949. The American-inspired WPs totalled some 755 engines, and they saw service throughout the entire country. Their rugged design proved suitable for Indian conditions, and they gave premium service until the end of steam.

BALDWIN INDUSTRIALS IN THE PHILIPPINES

0-6-0 and 0-6-0ST

A superb contrast between American industrials is seen here on the Hawaiian Philippine Company's system on Negros island in the Philippines in 1974, with a Baldwin 0-6-0ST of 1924 (left) along with No. 4, an 0-6-0 of 1920. These industrial workhorses operated for three shifts during the intensity of the sugar milling campaign, despite their having the aura of fairground engines on display. Their huge cabbage-stack smokestacks are designed to suppress the emission of sparks when burning bagasse. American railroading in miniature, complete with copper bells clanging with a musical resonance, combined with a glorious undulating wail of whippoorwill whistles.

INDIAN RAILWAYS XE
2-8-2

Indian Railway's XE-class 2-8-2s were the largest conventional engines working on the Indian subcontinent. They were introduced in 1928 as part of the X Series Standards, with examples coming from the Vulcan Foundry, Lancashire, and the legendary Clydeside shipbuilder Beardmore of Dalmuir. The XEs distinguished themselves for almost 50 years hauling 2,000-tonne coal trains over the hill regions of Bengal. Following mass withdrawals during the 1970s, a few were given major overhauls at Jamalpur Works and sold to industrial units, where some survived into the 1990s. When the last survivor ended its days at Korba Thermal Power Station in Madhya Pradesh, it was the last large British steam locomotive left in world service.

THE BIG MIKADOS OF INDIA
2-8-2

The most powerful conventional steam locomotives to work on the Indian subcontinent were the XE Mikados, delivered from the Vulcan Foundry, Lancashire, and Beardmore's Shipyard on Glasgow's Clydeside between 1928 and 1930. Unlike the American, the Mikado was not widely associated with Britain, and when it did appear it was primarily in export packages. The XEs totaled 58 locomotives, all built for the East Indian Railway. During the Second World War, further engines were acquired, and these were commissioned from Baldwin in the form of 40 engines classified AWE. It was inevitable that they should be "Americanized" and, although virtually identical in power, they make a fascinating visual contrast with their British sisters.

INDIAN RAILWAYS XD

The X Series Standards, supplied to the Indian subcontinent's 5'6"-gauge railroads during the 1920s, consisted primarily of Pacifics and Mikados. The most numerous class in the program were the XDs, which totaled 194 engines. Following their inception in 1929, the design was produced by four different builders. They were superb workhorses, often regarded as superior to the later and more powerful W.G. class 2-8-2s. The XDs could work 1,800-tonne coal trains over the 77 miles from Dornakal Junction to Vijayawada in 2½ hours.

15A, ARGENTINA
4-8-0

Argentina's 15A class consisted of eight oil-burning mixed-traffic locomotives, built in 1939 for the 5'6" gauge by the Vulcan Foundry in Lancashire. Their boilers, trucks, and tenders were identical to the 12K-class Pacifics built the same year. Originally the 15As were fitted with smoke deflectors, but these were later removed. Four examples were built with Caprotti valve gear, but this, too, was later removed in favor of Walschaerts. The 15As were very successful on the Buenos Aires to Mar del Plata night trains and particularly on the legendary fruit hauls from the Rio Negro valley. All were named, and some examples survived until the 1980s.

TEXAS TYPE, BRAZIL
2-10-4

One of the world's last Texas-type 2-10-4s highballs across the metals of Brazil's meter-gauge Teresa Cristina Railway at the head of a rake of empty coal wagons bound for the mine at Tubarao. These giants could reach speeds of up to 60 mph at the head of 1,800-tonne trains and represented American steam superpower scaled down to meter-gauge operation. Teresa Cristina was a coal-carrying railroad in southern Brazil, which remained steam-worked until the 1980s. Thirteen Texas types were included in the roster, having originally been built in 1940 by Baldwin and Alco for Brazil's mainline Central and Noroeste railways.

METER-GAUGE MACARTHUR

2-8-2

The meter-gauge MacArthur 2-8-2 was one of the most celebrated war engines in railroad history and, following the Second World War, it was notable for its widespread distribution around the world. MacArthur 2-8-2s were introduced by the United States Army Transportation Corps for operations in the Far East, being employed in India, Burma, Malaya, Thailand, and the Philippines. Most were built between 1942 and 1944, although a few were completed after the war. Postwar dispersal embraced Europe, Africa, and Latin America, rendering the MacArthur a truly international type. This example, classified MAWD, is pictured on India's North-East Frontier Railway in 1976.

SKYLINERS, TURKEY

2-10-0

The great days of North American railroading are recalled by this brace of Turkish State Railways Skyliners, which reigned supreme on the scenic, steeply graded route between Irmak and the Black Sea town of Zonguldak. A total of 88 of these massive 2-10-0s was built for the Turkish State Railways by Vulcan of Wilkes Barre between 1947 and 1949. The Irmak to Zonguldak line was also notable for employing Major Marsh's USATC S160 2-8-0s on banking duties at several locations.

MIKADO 310, SUDAN

Britain's most important legacy to Sudan was a vast and superbly run railroad network. This extended from Wadi Halfa, close to the Egyptian border in the north, to Wau, an incredible 1,457 miles to the south. Following Sudan's independence in 1956, the railroad underwent gradual deterioration to the great detriment of the nation. The system possessed a superb stud of blue-liveried 3'6" gauge locomotives which contrasted well with the golden tones of the surrounding desert. These 310-class Mikados date back to 1952 and, along with many of Sudan's locomotives, came from the North British Works in Glasgow.

S160, GREECE
2-8-0

The latter-day standard-gauge steam roster of Greece was full of fascinating diversities combining classic 0-10-0 and 2-10-0 designs. These were derived from the drawing board of the legendary Karl Golsdorf, C.M.E. of the Austrian State Railway; British-built locomotives from the Second World War; and a stud of Major Marsh's S160 2-8-0s, built for the United States Army Transportation Corps. Built to the British loading gauge, upward of 2,500 of these S160s were put into traffic from the American builders Baldwin, Alco, and Lima. These engines operated throughout the war zone, and following the conflict, some 50, classified Theta Gamma, were incorporated into Greek Railway stock. Survivors remained at work until the 1970s.

INDIAN RAILWAYS WT
2-8-4T

The WT-class 2-8-4Ts were the last word in suburban tanks on Indian Railways. The class consisted of 30 locomotives built between 1959 and 1967 at Chittaranjan Locomotive Works. These impressive locomotives had rapid acceleration and were powerful enough to haul heavy trains. Engine No. 14011 was built in 1965, and from its base at Rajamundry, where it is seen taking water, it worked cross-country passenger trains around the Godavri Delta in Andhra Pradesh.

ENGINES of WAR

The usefulness of railroads in a war zone was first recognized as early as the Crimea Campaign of 1854–56. By the end of the First World War, railroads were an intrinsic part of warfare, and hundreds of miles of narrow-gauge tracks led to the front lines. The Second World War also saw extensive use being made of the rail networks in all the theaters of conflict. The trains, under the most difficult of circumstances, moved munitions, troops, and casualties.

America built many field engines for use in the First World War war zone, as all the British manufacturers' capacity was fully utilized with the production of munitions. Again, during the Second World War, America supplied huge numbers of locomotives to both meter and standard gauges. These included the celebrated MacArthur 2-8-2s, along with Major Marsh's classic S160 2-8-2s, based on Stanier's 8Fs of the L.M.S. and conforming with the British loading gauge. Another important type was the USATC 0-6-0T. All three designs saw widespread distribution after the conflict.

In addition, America and Britain supplied postwar engines to conflict-shattered networks, including 1,323 14R mixed-traffic Mikados to France from the big three American builders and the famous "Liberation" 2-8-0s built by the Vulcan Foundry at Newton le Willows, Lancashire.

G.C.R. O4

2-8-0

In 1941, the call to arms came again for the Robinson O4 class 2-8-0s, and the British War Department despatched 92 of them to the Middle East. Some of these were the same engines that had been requisitioned in 1917, but this time they did not return home. After the Second World War, those that remained on the L.N.E.R. were generally confined to ex-G.C.R. routes, and withdrawals began in 1958. The class was extinct by 1966, with the notable exception of No. 63601, which was set aside for the National Collection and has since been restored to working order.

SUDAN RAILWAYS 220

4-6-2

Sudan's most numerous locomotive type were the 220-class Pacifics. First built in 1927, a total of 51 engines had come from North British by 1947, and the design was adopted as a standard by the British War Department, examples later being constructed for the Nyasaland and Trans-Zambesia railways, as well as the Western Australian Railways. In later years, these engines worked turnabout with the related 180- and 310-class Mikados, the last of which entered service in 1952. All three classes used the same boiler and other standard interchangeable parts.

S160, GREECE

2-8-0

The same specification as for the Riddles WD Austerities was laid down by the British Ministry of Supply for the American S160 class 2-8-0s, the only proviso being that they should conform to the British loading gauge. A design team headed by Major J.W. Marsh drew up a locomotive that could be built quickly and in large numbers by the big three American builders, Alco, Baldwin, and Lima, making use of standard parts. More than 800 of the class actually operated in Britain before being shipped to the war zone. Many stayed in Europe after the conflict, and some 50 engines ran in Greece until the 1970s.

U.S.A. NO. 30067

0-6-0T

American mass-production techniques were called on to build locomotives quickly for service during the Second World War. Two of the smaller American manufacturers, Vulcan and Porter, produced no fewer than 438 six-coupled switching tanks for shipment to Europe in 1942–43, and the engines were stored in Britain until required on the continent. At the end of the war, many remained unused, still in store at dumps around the country. A group of the engines stored at Newbury was inspected by Bulleid in 1946 and subsequently purchased by the Southern Railway for use in Southampton Docks.

L.N.E.R. J94

0-6-0ST

The Second World War brought a new customer for the Hunslet 18' saddle tank—the British War Department, which urgently needed switching locomotives for military use. The Hunslet design was preferred above the L.M.S. 3F 0-6-0T for this role, and no fewer than 377 were turned out by seven different builders after 1943. At the end of the war, the L.N.E.R. bought 75 of the engines to become their J94 class and scattered them widely round their docks and freight yards. But their finest moment came in B.R. days, when they were deployed on the tortuous curves and gradients of the Cromford & High Peak line in Derbyshire.

WD (WAR DEPARTMENT)
2-10-0

Having produced an excellent 2-8-0 for wartime service, Robert Riddles considered that a larger version would be desirable and expanded the design into a 2-10-0. Its great advantage was its bigger boiler with a wide firebox, allowing it to steam well on poor-quality coal. One hundred and fifty locomotives were built by North British in Glasgow, the first appearing in 1943, and many saw service on the L.M.S. and L.N.E.R. before being shipped abroad. Some were sent on to Egypt and Syria, and remained there after the war. The Egyptian contingent was later transferred to the Hellenic Railways of Greece, where they put in a further 28 years of work.

WD AUSTERITY
NO. 90459
2-8-0

Monochrome photography is somehow appropriate to record a filthy, work-stained WD 2-8-0. Consigned to the hardest and least glamorous work on the railway in England's industrial northeast, they slaved on in considerable numbers until displaced by B.R. Standard 9F 2-10-0s in the 1950s. No. 90459 is captured in characteristic grimy condition, filling up before its next turn of duty from an elegant North Eastern Railway water crane.

WD AUSTERITY NO. 1931

2-8-0

By 1943, the demand for heavy freight engines to assist the war effort was exceeding supply. The excellent L.M.S. Stanier 8F 2-8-0 was proving too expensive in materials and too time-consuming in construction, so a more economical solution was sought. In designing the WD 2-8-0, Robert Riddles took every opportunity to make the locomotive cheaper and quicker to manufacture. A parallel boiler with round-topped firebox replaced the Belpaire taper boiler of the 8F, while steel castings and forgings were eliminated by the use of fabricated components, and all other parts were kept as simple as possible.

WD NO. 73672

2-10-0

By far the largest group of WD 2-10-0s congregated in the Netherlands, where some continued working until the mid-1950s. One of these, the historic 1,000th war engine, is on display in the Utrecht Railway Museum. At the end of the war, Britain's railroads were less enthusiastic about adopting the returning WD 2-10-0s and preferred the eight-coupled version. Nevertheless, B.R. did take 25 of the class into stock as Nos. 90750–74. Several locomotives were retained by the British Army, and the last of these, No. 600 *Gordon*, can be seen on the Severn Valley Railway. Two of the Hellenic Railways locomotives have been repatriated to the North Yorkshire Moors Railway, where WD No. 73672 has been named *Dame Vera Lynn*.

WD AUSTERITY

2-8-0

Special attention was paid to making the WD 2-8-0 adaptable to the altered conditions of war service, so the boiler could quickly be converted for oil-firing without its removal from the engine. On the tender, the narrow coal bunker gave good rearward visibility when the engine was working tender-first, as it often had to do. The class immediately went into volume production by North British and Vulcan Foundry in 1943 and proved very successful in many spheres of operation, first in Britain before D-Day, then in France, Belgium, the Netherlands, and further afield.

ROW OF WD AUSTERITIES
2-8-0s

In all, around 900 WD 2-8-0s were built in a period of three years. After the war, 200 of them were taken into L.N.E.R. stock in 1946 and others were disposed of abroad. Eventually no fewer than 733 came into the possession of British Railways in 1948. They slogged on, grimy and neglected, until the 1960s, but in the end every single one went for scrap. One locomotive that had worked in the Netherlands and been sold in 1952 to the Swedish State Railways was discovered near the Arctic Circle, however, and brought back to work on the Worth Valley Railway.

USATC
0-6-0T

The Southern Railway took 14 of the USATC tanks into stock in 1947. To British eyes, their all-American appearance with features such as bar frames, boiler-top sandboxes, and stovepipe smokestacks made them look a little outlandish, but they were soon Anglicized with improved cabs, extended coal bunkers, and British-style regulator handles. Their short wheelbase made them ideal for dock switching, and they put in many years of useful work at Southampton. Two were painted in Southern green livery and one of these, B.R. No. 30064, was a popular choice for preservation and now operates on the Bluebell Railway in Sussex.

INDUSTRIAL LOCOMOTIVES

American industrial railways required specialized locomotives, often of designs quite different from those employed by mainline carriers. A factory or mill might need a low-profile switcher. As an engine of this sort needed to work in both directions with equal ease, a saddle-tank design, using either an 0-4-0 or 0-6-0 configuration was common.

Logging railroads needed high tractive effort at very low speed, especially when working over poorly built and often temporary track. This required an agile locomotive, and for this type of service several specialized types evolved using a flexible truck, powered by a geared drive instead of the conventional piston-and-drive-rod arrangement.

Industrial locomotives were isolated from the economics of mainline operations, which meant that they tended to survive longer than their larger cousins. As a result, by the time they were considered for retirement, steam preservation was more acute and relatively more industrial switchers were preserved. This was exactly what happened in Britain; the Industrial survived long after its mainline counterparts had disappeared and, accordingly, preservationists had the time to build up resources to save hundreds of them from the breaker's yard.

SHAY TYPE AT ELY-THOMAS LUMBER CO.

Three-truck

The most common type of logging locomotive was the Shay type, invented by Ephraim Shay in 1878, and from 1885 onward built by the Lima Machine Works of Lima, Ohio (later the Lima Locomotive works). Where the Pacific was built for power and speed, and the Mikado designed to move heavy mainline freight, the Shay was a specialized locomotive designed for hauling freight over poor track at very slow speeds and up steep gradients. This three-truck Shay was built in 1912 for the Erbacon & Summersville Railroad in West Virginia; 30 years later it was acquired by the Ely-Thomas Lumber Company, where it is pictured in the mid-1950s. A number of Shays have been preserved, including this one, which survives to this day at Pennsylvania Lumberman's Museum.

SHAY-TYPE LOGGING LOCOMOTIVE

In 1878, Ephraim Shay designed a geared steam locomotive for use on lightly built track such as that typically used by temporary timber hauling railroads. The earliest Shay types used a pair of vertically orientated cylinders to power a horizontal crankshaft that drove two pivoting two-axle trucks at each end of the locomotive. The locomotive was asymmetrical, with cylinders located in a bank on the engineer's side. Later Shays used a bank of three cylinders to power three two-axle trucks. Shays were manufactured by the Lima Machine Works of Lima, Ohio, and employed by logging railroads all across North America.

BEYER PEACOCK
GARRATT

0-4-4-0T

Britain's Beyer Peacock & Co. will best be remembered for their matchless Garratt articulated designs supplied to railroads across the world. Apart from those they built for the L.M.S. and L.N.E.R. companies, Beyer Peacock constructed four Garratts for industrial firms in Britain. The last survivor was *William Francis*, which was delivered new to Baddesley Colliery in Warwickshire and remained there throughout its working life. On withdrawal, it was fittingly set aside for preservation and may now be seen at Bressingham Steam Museum in Norfolk.

HEISLER LOGGING LOCOMOTIVE

Two-truck

Numerous timber railroads were built to harvest the forests of Appalachia in the eastern United States. These lines were of a relatively temporary nature and employed roughly built tracks and very steep gradients that required locomotives with flexible running gear, capable of maintaining high power at slow speeds. For this purpose, several manufacturers designed low-speed geared locomotives riding on trucks. The Heisler Locomotive Works specialized in machines such as this one belonging to the Meadow River Lumber Company, pictured near Rainelle, West Virginia, in the mid-1950s. It was built in October 1929 for Bostonia Coal & Clay Products of New Bethlehem, West Virginia. In 1967, after its days of timber service, it was saved from scrapping by the state of West Virginia and is today preserved at the Cass Scenic Railroad.

HUNSLET 16'

0-6-0ST

At the ironstone quarries of the East Midlands, the golden ore scooped up by the Ruston-Bucyrus steam excavator was loaded directly into standard gauge cars running over temporary tracks at the very lip of the quarry. Here at Nassington quarry, Peterborough, England, the two Hunslet 16' saddle tanks, *Jacks Green* and *Ring Haw* wait patiently for this operation to be completed, before blasting their way up the steep gradients to the mainline interchange sidings.

HUNSLET 18' AUSTERITY NO. 49

0-6-0ST

The industrial locomotive design produced in greatest numbers in Britain was without doubt the Austerity 0-6-0ST. Its origin can be found in the Hunslet 18' saddle tank, which with slight modification was chosen as the standard switching locomotive for the British Ministry of Supply in the Second World War. As well as the ex-WD engines sold to the L.N.E.R., the National Coal Board bought 47 and was so impressed that it immediately ordered a new batch from Hunslet.

HUNSLET AUSTERITY NO. 25

0-6-0ST

Eventually 234 locomotives were in service for the National Coal Board. Hunslet continued construction up to 1964, when the final pair of locomotives was delivered to the N.C.B. Over the years, several of the type have benefitted from such aids to efficiency and economy as Giesl ejectors, producer gas fueling, and underfeed stokers.

HUDSWELL CLARKE AT DESFORD COLLIERY

0-6-0ST

The family of inside-cylindered 0-6-0 saddle tanks produced by three manufacturers from Leeds, England—Manning Wardle, Hunslet, and Hudswell Clarke—could all trace their ancestry back to the designs of E.B. Wilson's Railway Foundry. They were the staple workhorses of British industry for more than a century, serving quarries, iron and steel works, coal mines, and a whole host of other manufacturing industries. In this timeless scene at Desford Colliery in Leicestershire, a classic Hudswell Clarke is hard at work against a backdrop of pithead winding gear.

R.S.H. 16' PROGRESS

0-6-0ST

When Robert Stephenson & Co. merged with Hawthorn Leslie in 1937, the new R.S.H. company perpetuated many of the attractive Hawthorn Leslie industrial locomotive designs, many of them dating back before the First World War. Such an engine is "Progress", built at Newcastle, England, in 1946 for colliery service in Leicestershire, first at Moira, then Measham, and finally at Cadley Hill, where she was maintained in first-class condition until the end of steam operations there.

R.S.H. AT LEICESTER POWER STATION

0-4-0ST

Although built by Robert Stephenson & Hawthorns of Newcastle, England, as recently as 1950, this smart little locomotive bears all the design hallmarks of its predecessor, Hawthorn Leslie & Co., being one of its standard four-coupled 12' saddle tanks, a design produced without significant alteration over a period of 40 years. The type found great favor within the electricity-generating industry, and many power stations including that at Leicester depicted here relied on their capacity for hard work until the advent of "merry-go-round" train operation.

ANDREW BARCLAY AT GOLDINGTON

0-4-0ST

Best known of the Scottish industrial locomotive builders, Andrew Barclay of Kilmarnock began manufacture in 1859. Its locomotives gained a reputation for toughness and hard work, virtues embodied in its popular 14' saddle tanks. Two of these were delivered new to Goldington Power Station in Bedfordshire in 1954, but were soon converted by the manufacturers to oil-burning. The reliability and economy achieved by the conversion kept both locomotives regularly employed at the power station for a quarter of a century.

ANDREW BARCLAY 16' AT DALMELLINGTON

0-4-0ST

The Andrew Barclay 0-4-0 saddle tanks on the Dalmellington system were the company's standard 16' product, but when working hard on the run to Pennyvenie Colliery in Ayrshire, Scotland, they could consume up to two tons of coal per shift—well in excess of the amount that could be carried on the footplate. Accordingly, they were each paired with an improvised tender made from a cut-down colliery car. This was a feature of operations on the N.C.B. Waterside system for many years, and the six-tonne capacity of these tenders enabled the engines to work for several days without re-coaling.

NDEX